The 5 Truths of Remarkable Leaders

Published in the United States by Twenty Third and
Parkway Publishing, Inc.

www.twentythirdandparkwaypublishing.com

ISBN 9781697983555

Printed in the United States of America

Contents

Acknowledgments

I'd like to think that no author writes a book alone. Even if you were the only one to put pen to paper, there was some form of support. It's a unique experience to take what's been rattling around inside your head and share with everyone else. There's absolutely no guarantee that your work will find a place, yet any author who believes in their work will continue on. So, I'd like to acknowledge all of those who came before me and all of those will follow along after me. Remember your work might one day change the world.

 With that covered, let's talk about the people who are much closer to me and went along for the ride these last two years. Beginning with my wife, Belle. Who rightfully looked at me sideways when I proclaimed to her *"I'm writing a book." S*he was patient and understanding when it came to the time I needed to dedicate to my writing. It's no understatement to say I wouldn't have been able to do this without her. And if I ever become a financial success, she'll be rewarded with regular trips to the beach to enjoy the sun and sand.

To my mother, for keeping me grounded throughout this entire process. Her occasional reminders that we don't all get to do what we'd like to do served to help me genuinely appreciate the opportunity that had come my way. For my son who is finding his way through his undergraduate career; this kid has already surpassed everything I'd hope he would accomplish. If you've ever heard me talk about him, you know the universe threw him a curveball from Day One. Yet he's managed to handle all of his struggles quite resolutely. He's the single greatest contribution I'll leave to the world.

For everyone who knew about this project and never said anything negative or kept their doubts to themselves. Thank you. I was going to do it any way, but it was refreshing not to have to deal with that type of energy while putting this all together. To everyone who showed love and support, I thank you as well. I can't name everyone - just know I didn't forget about you.

Finally, I have to thank the Heath Brothers. They authored a book entitled *"Switch, How to Change Things When Change is Hard"* that helped me both personally and professionally. In many ways that book inspired the style of this one. It's a great read and I recommend it to everyone. And If I've forgotten anyone it was not intentional.

Genesis

First, let me thank you for taking the time to select and read this book. There is no shortage of available material addressing concerns around management—and more specifically, leadership—as we head into the next decade. A decade where the changing global economy is sure to force companies to close their doors at an even higher rate than in previous eras. Once you factor in the variable that is the modern employee, the road ahead will become even more difficult to navigate. I wrote this because I want to help. I'd prefer to see more of my friends and former colleagues satisfied at the end of their workday instead of dreading the proposition of having to do it all over again, day after day after day. And trust me, they dread it.

But you know that already; your internal data and employee surveys have been telling you this for the last couple of years, if not longer. Yet for some reason, nothing's really changed. There's the standard lip service about wanting to create "the right culture," placing a high value on employees, offering open-door policies, and a bunch of other nice-sounding phrases. But the reality on the ground is actually quite dismal. Here are just a handful of data points to prove it:

According to a 2018 Association of Talent Development (Atd) skills gap survey:

- 61 percent of respondents identified managerial/supervisory skills as lacking inside their organization

- 52 percent of respondents identified leadership/executive-level skills as lacking inside their organization[1]

If we look at the 2018 Leadership Forecast compiled by Development Dimensions International (DDI), similarly alarming statistics come to light:

- 64 percent of respondents identified development of "Next Gen" leaders as their primary and largest concern
- 60 percent of respondents identified failure to attract/retain top talent as their second-largest concern[2]

How do we identify and implement a sustainable resolution to our employees' concerns if we can't even select, train, and retain the individuals who will ultimately be responsible for the employees? If we push further down the organizational chart and look at things from a front-line employee's standpoint, things become even more discouraging. I'm going to leverage one of the larger workforce studies around, a Gallup workforce study from 2013, to illustrate the problem:

According to the study, which surveyed employees at various companies:

---

[1] "Bridging the Skills Gap: Workforce Development and the Future of Work," December 2018, pg. 12, Amy Souza and Kristen Fyfe-Mills Nancy Harvin, Jerry Kaminski, Cristina Masucci, and Paul Smith.

[2] 2018 Leadership Forecast Development Dimensions International (DDI), pg. 4, "Global Leadership Forecast 2018 - 25 Research Insights to Fuel Your People Strategy," 2018, pg. 4 Rebecca L. Ray

- 11 percent of respondents report being engaged in the period between 2008 and 2009
- 13 percent of respondents reported being engaged in the period between 2011 and 2012[3]

Fast-forward to a 2018 Gallup study on the US workforce:

- 33 percent of respondents, all of whom were US employees, reported being engaged at work between 2016 and 2017[4]

Stay with me—we're almost done. Heading back to the Gallup study, these three statistics come screaming off the page:

- Less than 25 percent of employees STRONGLY AGREED that their performance was managed in a way that motivated them to do outstanding work[5]
- Only 22 percent of employees STRONGLY AGREED that leadership of their organization had a clear direction for it
- A paltry 15 percent of employees STRONGLY AGREED that the leadership of their organization made them enthusiastic about the future[6]

---

[3] "State of the Global Workplace - Employee Engagement Insights for Business Leaders Worldwide," Ed O'Boyle, Jim Harter PhD, pg. 12

[4] "State of the American Workplace," Gallup pg. 17

[5] "State of the American Workplace," Gallup pg. 6

[6] "State of the American Workplace," Gallup pg. 9

You may be wondering, why all the doom and gloom? I want you to be fully abreast of the challenges you're taking on as a leader. I want you to know that whether you're a first-time shift leader at a casual-dining restaurant, a tenured mid-level manager for a Fortune 500 company, a small business owner, or a senior-level manager, how you choose to lead has a direct impact on the members of your team. What you do will impact how they perform, their tenure with your company, their mental (and possibly physical) health. You need to decide right now if you are up to this challenge or not, because the real truth is this: *Little of what you do as a leader is about you. It is about those who make up your team.*

I know this because for a long time I was the employee. I sat and watched as my career and the careers of my colleagues were tended to once a year, when performance reviews were due. I watched as committed people did everything that was asked of them, only later to be told their efforts were worth an astonishing three percent raise at the end of the year. *Three percent!* Over the last five years I was fortunate to have the opportunity to interview and learn from a number of people (small business owners, academics, CEOs) who've helped expand my perspective on leadership. While each of them had their own distinct approach to leadership, there were a number of similarities between them. Keeping people first and remaining true to your vision were the most common.

Two years ago, I wrote a post for LinkedIn on this very topic, "*The 5 Truths all management teams need to hear.*"

The post came about after watching a docu-series on Amazon Prime about US Army Special Forces. At the beginning of each episode, the narrator would spell out the 5 Truths. It took three episodes before those truths actually sank in. Intrigued, I decided to do some research. Eventually I found what I was looking for: a 1987 report Colonel John Allen made to the House of Representatives' Special Operations Panel of the Readiness Subcommittee of the Committee on Armed Services.

In the report Colonel Allen outlined a philosophy that would come to be known as "The SOF Truths." It would be implemented by the US Special Operations Command as an overarching philosophy on how to "manage" the most elite warriors in the US military. I had struck gold. That very night, I penned the article that would eventually give birth to this book. At the time I had no indication of what would follow.

Over the course of the next six months, the engagement was incredible: nearly 20,000 views and hundreds of shares and likes. But more importantly and ultimately more telling was the feedback from readers. People from all around the world took the time to let me know that they agreed with what I'd written. I'd highlighted this rather rare military ethos that's been hidden away and leveraged it, explaining to managers what was needed if they wanted to elevate their teams from okay to exceptional. It was clear the message was being received by the right people. So I decided to continue the conversation and expand it beyond a single platform.

I stated earlier that I wrote this because I wanted to help, and I genuinely mean that. I know we can do better than having only one-third of the workforce actively engaged. We can do better than having employees feel as if their careers are a secondary concern to profits, earnings per share, and quarterly forecasts.

As you read through this book, you will notice these sentiments echoed in different ways through each chapter. You will be asked to listen, empower, recognize and reward. To complete simple steps that don't require a new budget or approval from the board of directors. You don't need outside consultants or anything extraordinary —you simply need to be ready to serve. These are things you are already wired to do as a human. Hopefully, you've been the recipient of such actions at some point in your career. And now it's your turn to give back what was given or should have been given to you. This is the role you stepped into, and this is what it requires. These are *"The 5 Truths of Remarkable Leaders"*.

Truth I

Humans are more important than hardware. *{People, ideas and technology in that order}*

"Technology is a useful servant but a dangerous master." - Christian Lous Lange

Few of us are immune to the advances of technology. So much so, we now live in a marketplace that insists tech is the only way to move forward. Automate, automate, automate: This is the mantra of the twenty-first century. The jury is still out as to whether this will be better for the consumer. In the workplace, however, those of you in leadership roles will have to address the ever-increasing presence of technological disruption in your daily activities and those of your team.

Depending on what report you read, the displacement of the human worker is expected to begin in earnest anywhere between now and the next decade or so. According to a January 2019 study from the Brookings Institution, approximately thirty-six million American workers currently have jobs with "high exposure" to automation ("high exposure" meaning at least 70 percent of their tasks could soon be performed by machines using current technology).[7] In this new reckoning kiosks will replace cashiers, and RFID stickers will provide data on purchases, shelf life, and a product's popularity. Stores will become cashless environments that simply deduct purchases directly from your banking account.

If you take automation proponents' word for it, the benefits of automation will be significant:

- Fewer people, fewer mistakes.

---

[7] https://www.brookings.edu/wp-content/uploads/2019/01/2019.01_BrookingsMetro_Automation-AI_Report_Muro-Maxim-Whiton-FINAL-version.pdf, in "Executive Summary" section.

- Automation is easier to scale, therefore lowering operating cost and increasing revenue.
- At any rate, the argument goes, everyone else is doing it, so other companies will need to follow suit to remain competitive.

As these changes take hold it will be very easy to get swept up in a mindset that seeks to minimize human interaction for the reported benefits of automation. However, in this race to always have the latest and greatest thing, the most significant factor in your company's success is being downplayed. In case you're wondering, that factor is *people*. From my long experience in the work world, it's always been people and it will always be people. Show me any company that is doing well, and I will show you an individual or group of individuals who form the backbone of that company and are genuinely responsible for its success.

The original iPhone, while groundbreaking, wasn't a perfect device. But Steve Jobs still convinced you to buy it. The same thing can be said of Microsoft or even Atari—you could see the potential in their original iterations, but what inevitably sold you on them were the people behind the tech: the charismatic founder, the off-center marketing guru, and/or the financial whiz who kept the company floating when there was little to no revenue. People will always be the most important ingredient in your recipe for significance. If you don't believe me, keep reading. (And even if you do, you'll probably still get a lot out of the ideas I cover.)

* * *

The Blair Witch Project

For the first example, let's rewind all the way back to the summer of 1999, when a small-budget film left a massive impact on the movie industry. On July 16 of that year, the independently produced and directed *Blair Witch Project* was released. Movie audiences were not prepared for what they saw in the theater. And Hollywood certainly wasn't prepared for what they saw in box office receipts. Writer- directors Eduardo Sánchez and Daniel Myrick took roughly two years to complete the film, an ultra-low-budget horror flick. A labor of love, it was the only film they felt they could create given their limited resources. While many people would later parody the movie for its shaky camera movements, documentary feel, sparse script, and unknown actors, those exact factors were responsible for turning the movie into a cultural phenomenon.

"*Blair Witch* was born out of necessity, the cheaper the better. It was one of these things [where] every negative of low-budget filmmaking became a positive for us. Indie films rarely have stars; we couldn't have had stars, because people needed to be unrecognizable. Lighting is a big expense in movies; we couldn't do lighting because it would be fake, [and] you don't have lighting in the woods. Same thing with audio quality. It's terrible; well audio quality is terrible, it's a shitty camera. So everything that was a detriment to filmmaking became a positive for us. That's how we knew the idea was right."[8]

To give you some context, there were several other movies in the same thriller/horror genre released the same year that competed directly or indirectly with *The Blair Witch Project. The Sixth* Sense, *Sleepy Hollow, Stir of*

[8] Interview with the author.

Echoes, and *End of Days* are just a few. Each of these movies, however, had a certifiable star: Bruce Willis, Johnny Depp, Kevin Bacon, or the Terminator himself, Arnold Schwarzenegger. Each also had a typical Hollywood budget for production and marketing. So, riddle me this: Which of these movies outperformed *The Blair Witch Project* in total box office receipts?

Only one, in fact. *The Sixth Sense*, with Bruce Willis, was a runaway box office hit, grossing nearly $670 million— but it also had a budget a thousand times larger than *Blair Witch*'s. I'll repeat that for clarity's sake: The budget for *The Sixth Sense* was a reported $55 million. The budget for *Blair Witch* was reported to be around $60,000. For its effort, the latter grossed approximately $250 million in ticket sales. That is what we call a return on investment. So even though *The Sixth Sense* had a larger box office showing, when you factor in the budgets of the two movies, *Blair Witch* outperformed it in remarkable fashion.

Additionally, despite all the success *The Sixth Sense* enjoyed, including tremendous critical acclaim, its lasting impact simply does not compare to *The Blair Witch Project's*. The number of movies that blatantly copied the *Blair Witch* formula and format is so large, it essentially reintroduced the world to a once-lost subgenre of horror movies called "found footage films." That's impact. Everyone remembers the scene where Heather, teary-eyed and nose runny, looks down into the camera and apologizes to her family. That scene is now part of cinematic history. It *is* pop culture.

At this point, you may be wondering: What does all this have to do with people and technology? *"The Blair Witch Project* was a one-hit wonder with a forgettable sequel. I run a call center where the agents troubleshoot technical issues. I use Salesforce to keep track of our clients. I don't have that type of creative freedom. There's nothing in this lesson about a movie that will help me with my team."

Let's take a closer look and see if that's really the case.

Team Goals

Sánchez and Myrick had to convince everyone involved with the movie that it merited their very best efforts even though they couldn't guarantee that it would even be released. Imagine you're a (low-paid) actor working on this set—would you initially give it your all under these circumstances? By definition, this is what leadership is about: laying out a vision and convincing everyone on your team that they have a part to play in bringing the vision into being. Think about what it took to keep everyone on task after long days of wandering the woods of rural Maryland while carrying their own equipment. There was no craft services or air-conditioned trailers. No wardrobes or stunt doubles. No fans or red carpets at the premiere—just multiple days of grueling, guerilla-style moviemaking.

Ultimately, everyone's hard work paid off, and *The Blair Witch Project* was picked up for distribution after its initial screening at the Sundance Film Festival in 1998. While it received just a single offer, that offer was more than enough. Sánchez and Myrick had' accomplished something only a very few other productions teams had managed to: a film that would alter the course of film making to follow. If you're having trouble with team cohesion and direction, ask yourself if you've looked at the possibility that your team simply isn't on the same page when it comes to direction, vision, and goals. If that's the case, the next question you should ask should be: Who's responsible for that? Leaders who can clearly articulate team goals that are larger than any single person are much more likely to motivate their team to meet these goals. And you should consistently deliver results in unique and unexpected ways.

Money Ain't a Thing

Though the filmmakers did receive some financial support, the bulk of the movie was self-funded. Because of this, frugality became a necessity. Sánchez's quote from earlier describes how he and Myrick used what they had available to make the movie—no less, and definitely no more. Despite their meager circumstances, they didn't put the movie on hold until they could get more advanced equipment. Along the way they figured out how to transform the presumed negatives into positives. It would have been easy for them to stop and wait until they had more financial backing before continuing, but they weathered the ups and downs because of their belief in the project. The result, as we know, turned out to be amazing.

Workplaces can draw big lessons from the filmmakers' example. Your team will always ask for the latest and greatest tools, and while the funds for them may not come out of your own pocket, they will likely come out of a budget assigned to your team or department. So it's a given that it will always be important to keep operating costs low. That doesn't mean, however, your team can't tackle the big jobs. It doesn't mean they can't use it as a test bed for new ideas. All the funding in the world can't cover for a mediocre product or performance.

Both Sánchez and Myrick recognized early that the more creative aspects of the movie were the areas where they could have the greatest impact. Essentially, their budget restraints forced them to find other ways to make a memorable movie. The script was largely improvised by the actors during each scene. They were provided an outline of the scene but left to their own devices to create the dialogue. So what you saw in the final product lent more authenticity to the story and even made it believable, which viewers clearly appreciated.

As part of their (barely funded) marketing campaign, the night before the movie's premiere at Sundance the directors created missing-person flyers and posted them on the streets of Salt Lake City, where Sundance takes place. This was viral marketing way before we became familiar with the term. Additionally, Sánchez created a journal for the lead female character, Heather, and regularly posted parts of it on their website to keep fans engaged until the movie premiered. We all know the famous quote "necessity is the mother of invention"—well, these are just a few examples that show it to be true. In the case of *The Blair Witch Project*, a tight budget fostered the environment for incredibly creative things to happen. What innate and undiscovered talents exist on your team? Are you putting those to use? As the leader, you should be receptive to creative ideas from your team when your budget doesn't allow you to do everything you want. With an open mind and some effort, you may discover a new method that allows your team to break new ground. *The Blair Witch Project* teaches us that the final product is far more important than the tools used to create it.

In 2015 I interviewed Sánchez for an article I was working on. I asked him if he felt we were becoming too reliant on technology.

"Yeah, absolutely," he said. "There's excellent content out there obviously, but we just get wrapped up with the gadgetry—at the end of the day you still have to tell a good story. If you don't have a good story, people are going to tell you. You will see very quickly . . . you could spend $100 million on a movie, you could have every great actor, great directors, and writers, and if something doesn't click, nobody is going to want to see it."

True, *your* final product is probably not going to be a movie, but this serves as a stellar example of what can be done when everyone on a team is dialed in and understands the end goal. I'm sure there have been cases where you've seen the latest CRM installed and it did nothing to change the effectiveness of say, your sales team. If Sales doesn't see the value in the CRM, guess what: They won't use it. Or worse, they expect it to be the "silver bullet" that will increase sales and come to rely on it exclusively, forgetting that sales still requires a human touch.

New tools can become a crutch that distracts us into focusing our attention externally, instead of looking internally and diagnosing outward. If your team is constantly asking for new tools, ask them what they would do if their current ones were not available. How would they get things done? Don't be afraid to challenge them and see what comes of it. I'm confident your team could find a way forward if this happened. All of which is to say: It's not about the tools—it's about the team.

* * *

Just in Time

The next example illustrates the long-term negative impact of our reliance on emerging technology, especially when it comes at the expense of understanding our employees. Not too surprisingly, this trend has its roots in the world of manufacturing; to be more specific, "just-in-time" (JIT) manufacturing. Under this system, a manufacturer will produce goods only to meet demand instead of keeping a surplus on hand. This supposedly leads to a reduction in wasted materials and time and minimizes excess inventory; the intent is to reduce overall costs by using resources only when they are needed. If there's an uptick in demand you bring in more resources; if there's a decline in demand you let go of or use fewer resources.

By the mid-2000s, however, the concept had been adopted by companies in the wider economy, and with particular zeal by retail chains, who took to scheduling employees using nonstandard schedules. In practice this meant that employees were generally expected to work at any time throughout the day, as their schedules were subject to change with little prior notice. Unlike the rest of the work world, which operated using regular shifts or preplanned schedules, these men and women had to react to the fluctuations in foot traffic throughout the day. On the surface, the JIT method is a unique way to address labor costs during the various swings in the retail cycle without creating any unnecessary turnover. If a store has minimal foot traffic, then being fully staffed means it is falling behind, because the amount of revenue being generated doesn't offset the labor costs. Conversely, if you don't have enough staff to assist customers during a high-traffic period, then you are likely missing sales opportunities that would lead to more revenue. So, what's an employer supposed to do?

Change the way employees are being scheduled, of course. That's an easy prospect if the store's busiest days are always the same times and days of the week. This becomes more difficult, though, if an ordinarily slow day becomes unusually busy. The more erratic these changes are, the more difficult they will be to resolve. How does the staff keep up if they are shorthanded? Or, on the other side of the spectrum, what should be done when the store is fully staffed, yet foot traffic is nonexistent? Any retail organization can survive a few days like this. If it happens too often, however, concern will begin to grow. In either case, it can create a headache for store managers, who must keep a vigilant eye on their P&L.

For many employers, the answer to this dilemma was scheduling software that could ensure the store would always be staffed at the appropriate level. There would be no more worries about sending people home if foot traffic was down or scrambling to find people if the store was suddenly busy. The software was referred to as "workforce optimization," and its party piece was a dataset drawn from previous year's sales trends, economic indicators, changes in weather, and political pressures. The intention was to make a perfectly predictable schedule that could provide real-time information for managers and empower them to make adjustments as variables changed.[9]

What's wrong this approach, you might be tempted to ask. It's using critical data about the store to predict traffic and outline what its staffing levels should be. Isn't this perfectly optimal? Not exactly. There was one variable that was missing from all the data that went into the workforce optimization tool: the employee.

If we take a minute to consider their perspective, it should be easy to see where this approach was going to run into trouble. When you look at labor costs, you see a number. That number gets plugged in with other numbers and eventually, you get a schedule. What you aren't seeing in that labor cost is the individual and all the variables that come along with that individual. Do they drive to work or take the bus? Are they married or

---

[9] "Shift Change: 'Just-in-Time' Scheduling Creates Chaos for Workers." NBCNews.com, NBCUniversal News Group, 10 May 2014, www.nbcnews.com/feature/in-plain-sight/shift-change-just-in-time-scheduling-creates-chaos-workers-n95881.

single? Do they have school-age children, infants, or college-bound kids? Are they caring for senior parents or other family members? All these seemingly innocuous variables directly impact the availability of any employee, yet in most cases, none of this was accounted for. So you can only imagine the chaos that ensued when companies deployed this new scheduling system in the real world. A world where childcare, public transportation, school, and other obligations aren't run by a "just-in-time" schedule, but a completely predictable and regular one.

For people employed by multiple companies, this system created a massive scheduling nightmare. "What we see is that workers are being used as a variable cost and have no choice," Sasha Hammad, executive director of the Retail Action Project, an employee advocacy organization, explained in a 2014 NBC News report on the JIT trend. "When workers need something to change, they are told that the system can't change it."[10] Take for example Walmart, who adopted a system like this in 2007. With work hours allocated based on the level of store traffic each day, some workers were scheduled for two-hour or four-hour shifts that could come at any time, day or night.[11]

In a 2014 report, the Retail Action Project inquired about the experiences of New York City retail workers,

---

[10] Ibid.

[11] Tsosie, Claire. "Just-In-Time Scheduling: Does It Really Save Companies Money?" NerdWallet, 24 Sept. 2014, www.nerdwallet.com/blog/finance/time-scheduling-save-companies-money/.

surveying over two hundred people and conducting in-depth interviews with forty-four. Although some interviewees said they were happy with their jobs, the overwhelming majority expressed frustration with their erratic work hours and workplace expectations, which they felt were unfair. "This is the worst job I've ever had," said retail worker Melvin. "And this is the worst pay I've ever had. I just try to give my best performance, just so I can use that and go somewhere else. This is not a place for growth."[12]

An earlier report by the organization in 2011 found similarly chaotic scheduling practices:

- only 17 percent of workers they surveyed had a set schedule
- 30 percent knew their schedule more than a week out
- 50 percent were aware of their schedule within a week [13]

To stabilize the staffing levels in their stores, employers threw their employees' lives into disarray with no real means to address it. This is an almost perfect example of the cure being worse than the disease. How well do you think a store filled with stressed out, precarious workers will perform? This is what happens when people count on a tool to address a problem that is far

---

[12] "Short Shifted." http://retailactionproject.org/wp-content/uploads/2014/09/ShortShifted_report_FINAL.pdf

[13] "Discounted Jobs." http://retailactionproject.org/wp-content/uploads/2012/01/FINAL_RAP.pdf

more complicated than it seems on the surface. So what could employers have done differently? Well, quite a bit.

P&L Blues

I will suggest to you that the core problem isn't staffing—it's lost revenue. The surface argument is that the stores have too much overhead in the form of labor costs, but missed opportunities to generate revenue are what most retailers should actually be focused on. Can you remember a time when you went into a store where there were shoppers and what appeared to be a full staff, but there was very little activity going on? I know I've seen it on a few occasions. What's behind the lack of sales activity? If the store is fully staffed, we can safely say that service time shouldn't be an issue. Which means there are other factors at play. Consider the way that you're greeted when you enter most stores. Does it lead to a definitive sales process? Or does it leave shoppers to mill about randomly? Interactions that are designed to guide shoppers through an engaging sales process are more likely to generate more sales opportunities.

When the sales opportunities increase, we all know sales will increase. And when sales increase, revenue can increase. So, is the question really about the quantity of the staff or the quality of the staff? We'll discuss the notion of "quality vs. quantity" more in a later chapter, but for now, I want you to hold onto the idea that *a well-trained, motivated, engaged staff will always outperform one that isn't any of these things*, regardless of staffing levels. Obviously, there are some cases where having a consistently understaffed business is at the root of missed opportunities, but in most cases, I'd ask you to think long and hard about what the staff in the store could be doing to increase sales. Which leads us to . . . you guessed it, store leadership.

If you accepted my earlier premise that the real issue is lost revenue, then we also must discuss how stores are managed. Which, of course, brings us back to automated scheduling. If the manager of a store is forced to spend the bulk of their day referring to computer-generated schedules and making staffing adjustments on the fly, how much time do they have to focus on the other things that are critical for the store to reach its sales goals? Not a lot, most likely. Yet again we see how a supposed fix can end up creating new problems.

2-D in a 3-D World

If we look at all the variables that go into a retail store's success, it's clear that staffing is only one of many. Does the sales process match the clientele? Is the right merchandise in the store? Have the right people been selected as retail consultants in the store? Are the goods priced to be profitable or simply drive traffic? All these variables will play a role in daily sales numbers. So if your management team is held captive to a scheduling program that only addresses one variable, when do they have the time to investigate these other incredibly important factors?

When management teams see their staff as simply variables or entries in a log, they become two-dimensional. They are no longer people with lives and responsibilities, but "plug & play" options to be turned off and on indiscriminately. And when you reduce a three-dimensional person into a two-dimensional software input, that missing human dimension will become a problem. Solutions like JIT scheduling tend to be focused more on short-term returns instead of long-term problem-solving. Accordingly, as time goes on, the negative results have become increasingly clear. "Frontline managers are squeezed," Susan Lambert, a University of Chicago researcher who studies low-wage workers, told NBC News in 2014. "The managers are the ones who are held accountable for keeping a ratio for sales or traffic and the number of hours. Sometimes they look at [schedules] every half hour and make adjustments all day long."[14] The workers live in a world of school closings, car accidents, elderly parents, and countless other unpredictable events. The managers live in a world of hourly sales reports and labor costs. Does this sound like a winning combination to you?

Penny Wise, Pound Foolish

Now let's talk about the primary unintended consequence of implementing these workforce optimization systems: increased costs. "When employers take a purely in the moment, tactical approach to demand for labor activity without regard for any other considerations, they run the risk of increasing overall costs," HR expert and Deloitte

---

[14] "Shift Change: 'Just-in-Time' Scheduling Creates Chaos for Workers." NBCNews.com, NBCUniversal News Group, May 10, 2014, www.nbcnews.com/feature/in-plain-sight/shift-change-just-in-time-scheduling-creates-chaos-workers-n95881.

consultant Lisa Disselkamp told NBC News. The increased costs she is referring to come in the form of lower productivity and increased overhead. Unsustainable scheduling inevitably results in higher turnover, missed shifts, and low worker morale.[15] According to a 2012 study by the Center for American Progress think tank, people working in lodging, food services, leisure, hospitality, and retail—some of the industries most affected by irregular shift work—reported the highest rates of employees quitting their jobs at 37%.[16] These high rates come with a hefty price tag. The CAP study found that the cost of replacing employees with salaries under $30,000 was about 16 percent of a worker's salary.[17]

That's real money by the way, not monopoly money. According to Glassdoor, the average base pay for a retail sales associate is $24,809 per year, with roughly $3,800 in bonus pay and commissions, which means the cost to replace an employee whose salary caps out around $30,000 is $4,800 for the employer. In other words, a good majority of the workforce inside a clothing, electronics, or big-box store becomes far more costly to replace than keep. And this isn't even accounting for the revenue that's lost while training for new hires. When you begin to take all of this into account, one thing starts to become very clear: Even for companies with a

---

[15] Ibid.

[16] https://cdn.americanprogress.org/wp-content/uploads/2012/11/CostofTurnover.pdf pg 3

[17] https://cdn.americanprogress.org/wp-content/uploads/2012/11/CostofTurnover.pdf pg 2

part-time workforce, the cost of employee turnover can outweigh most productivity or sales gains any just-in-time scheduling methodology provides.

This shows, as I mentioned earlier, that an overreliance on technology tricks us into focusing our attention outward instead of inward. It allows us to create a scenario where the root of our failures is tied to a set of circumstances for which some new tool is sure to correct. This way, we never have to accept our role in the shortcomings that plague our teams. Or so we think.

In this chapter I've given you two different and deeply illustrative examples. In the first, we looked at a case where older technology and a limited budget were not allowed to hinder a project that would go on to generate hundreds of millions of dollars in revenue and breathe life back into a forgotten genre of film. In the second we saw how the short-sighted implementation of a tool that was designed to stabilize costs ended up raising them. As counterintuitive as it may seem, tools, technology, and "things" can't by themselves make your team better. Now before all the Six Sigma black belts come looking for me armed with reams of data, I will agree that a company can become more efficient with the introduction of new tools and technology. Your company may even become more profitable in the short term. But the success of your teams—regardless of their size, location, or function—will always be driven by the individuals who make them up.

When you as a manager or department head lose sight of that, you risk heading down a path that devalues the one thing your competitors cannot duplicate: your people.

Truth II

Quality beats quantity.

{A small team of people who are carefully selected, trained, and led are preferable to a larger team, which may have members not up to the task}

"Look for quality rather than quantity. Let your guiding rule be not how much, but how good. A thing you do not want is expensive at any price."

- Unknown

We spent the previous chapter discussing the importance of the living-and-breathing humans that make up your teams and how indispensable they really are. Now we're going to talk about the size of your teams and the quality of the talent on them. In most cases you don't get to choose when it comes to these two factors. Instead, you walk into a team that's already been set up. Your job at a minimum is to keep the team from losing ground, but ideally, you'll be tasked with moving everyone forward. The team could be made up of five people or fifty people. They may be highly motivated or deeply dissatisfied. None of that will stop the deadlines. So let's kick this off with a starting question: Is there an inherent benefit to a larger team?

The answer may seem obvious. If you've got more people, the numbers mean you can get more work done, right? It's easy enough to argue in favor of more bodies when it comes to getting stuff done. There's a school of thought, however, that suggests a smaller, more committed workforce is a better use of resources in the long run. To help you think about this more deeply, consider the following scenario: Your department is faced with a large, important project. Do you assemble your entire team to complete it? Or do you select the employees who are highly invested in completing it? It's a difficult decision all the way around. You don't want to ruffle feathers and alienate members of your team, but the work must be done. Correctly.

I will argue in this chapter that the second option is preferable, that keeping your team small and focused is often the best way to meet your goals. We are going to look at two examples that show how this works in the real world.

* * *

AMG

If you're an auto enthusiast or even a casual observer you've no doubt seen the following letters on the back of a few Mercedes-Benz sedans and coupes: AMG. These letters represent Hans Werner Aufrecht, Erhard Melcher, and the city of Großaspach, Germany, where both men hail from. AMG is Mr. Hyde to Mercedes's Dr. Jekyll. While Mercedes is world-renowned for building luxury vehicles that can cross continents at triple-digit speeds with amazing levels of comfort and next-generation safety, AMG has enhanced that comfort and safety with massive engines, turning those same cars into opulent brutes—think of an iron fist in a leather-lined glove.

It all began in the development department of Mercedes's motorsports division, where Aufrecht and Melcher were engineers during the 1960s. After Mercedes pulled the plug on the division, the men decided to work on an engine for the 300SE model in their spare time. This engine would debut in 1965 at the German Touring Car Championship, which it went on to win ten times.[18] In 1967, buoyed by their winning prototype, both men left their roles at Mercedes to start their own venture, "Aufrecht Melcher Großaspach Ingenieurbüro, Konstruktion und Versuch zur

---

[18] https://www.mercedes-amg.com/en/driving-performance/history.html

Entwicklung von Rennmotoren" ("Aufrecht Melcher Großaspach engineering firm, design and testing for the development of racing engines").

Jump ahead to 1971. Their next major test is the Spa 24 Hours, a twenty-four-hour endurance race at the wonderful and historic Circuit de Spa-Francorchamps in Belgium. They would once again taste victory, this time with their AMG Mercedes 300SEL 6.8, which won its class and finished second place overall. Keep in mind the 300SEL of that period was a full-size luxury sedan, the equivalent of a modern-day S-class. Which means this was not a small feat; in fact, just *finishing* the race was considered a victory for many teams. For Aufrecht and Melcher's entry to win its class and finish second in overall scoring, and do it without the backing of a major manufacturer, is the type of accomplishment anyone in motorsports would kill to claim. This was the launching pad from which AMG would build a highly respected name in motorsports.

In 1986, AMG provided the US market with its first taste of automotive excess. The offering was a vehicle dubbed "the Hammer"—a 300E sedan with the choice of 5.0 or 6.0 liter V8 stuffed into its engine bay. It was a brutal luxury sedan that could give most *sports cars* a run for their money. Amazingly, up to this point the team behind all this success consisted of no more than one hundred or so employees. Yet their impact far outweighed their company footprint. We all know that cars for the most part are depreciating items, and only the rarest of them manage to hold their value or appreciate over time. Now allow me to present for the jury's consideration a 1989 Widebody 560 SEC AMG, a vehicle that would have a total build of approximately fifty cars. This model existed prior to the full-on merger between AMG and Mercedes. Brand-new, this vehicle would have retailed for something in the neighborhood of $200K. 'In March of 2019, RM Sotheby's recorded a sale for approximately $180k. [19] Thirty years later this vehicle had depreciated by about 10 percent. Your average midsize sedan will depreciate by more than that in the first twenty-four *months* of ownership.

Over the next thirty years, AMG would continue growing their product line and motorsport experience. The 190E won 50 DTM (Germany's Touring Car Masters) races between 1988 and 1993. Once the '90s came about AMG products were sold through the Mercedes-Benz dealer network. At the tail end of the decade, Daimler-Benz took a majority stake in AMG and placed Aufrecht in charge of the automaker's motorsport department and the management of the German touring car team. In 2005, the remaining shares of AMG were acquired by Daimler, making the singularly focused upstart company a prized member of the Daimler family.[20]

What lessons can we learn from the growth of AMG from a two-man operation in a shed to a global motorsports powerhouse and in-house tuner for Mercedes Benz? Plenty, in fact.

---

[19] https://rmsothebys.com/en/auctions/am19/amelia-island/lots/r0026-1989-mercedes-benz-560-sec-amg-60-wide-body/733351.

[20] https://www.mercedes-amg.com/en/driving-performance/history.html.

Finding True North

When used properly small teams have several advantages over large teams. The first is a clear line of sight to the end goal. Mercedes likely employs hundreds of engineers to design the latest generation of engines. These engineers will be aware of all types of consumer preferences, governmental regulations, and technology. However, those teams are focused on the broader buying public, the 80 percent in the 80–20 rule. And with that will inevitably come compromise. Of course, their customers want performance . . . but fuel economy is important as well. There are always emissions standards, too. And even though Mercedes is a luxury brand, pricing can never be dismissed. So even with hundreds of engineers on staff and all the resources any engineer could ever want, sustained profitability requires a broader focus.

In comparison, AMG was started by two engineers who were exceptionally focused on building racing engines. Cost, emissions, and standard driving regulations were of no real concern. These men wanted an engine that would make them contenders on the world racing stage— period. So even though they had minimal resources, they were able to make strides in engine development in areas where Mercedes couldn't afford to explore. They never lost sight of what they wanted to accomplish. Their product wasn't watered down. Everything in *their* business centered around the engines. In the rare case when an employee forgot why they were working at AMG, all they had to do was look down at a nearby workstation and immediately be reminded of the company's mission.

Daimler is a massive worldwide company, responsible for several brands across multiple continents. Mercedes-Benz is just one of those brands. Can you imagine the number of meetings and conference calls it would take to develop a new engine platform? The process of creating a new one typically begins several years before it's released, and every department wants to have some say in the development. The marketing team will want something that sounds sexy, and the performance guys will inevitably want to beat their competitors at all costs. Don't forget the safety squad, either. Finally, there are the accountants. Everyone is lobbying for what's important to them, a process makes design, development, and application a real headache.

Aufrecht and Melcher weren't bogged down with the same levels of red tape and politics that you typically see with larger teams. While admittedly I was never present during their early years, I imagine that in 1965 any engineer who wanted to stuff a massive V-8 inside a luxury sedan and race it wasn't the type of person who was going to be fond of budget meetings, conference calls, and consumer focus groups. What would have taken Daimler or Mercedes three or more years to develop, test, and deploy took AMG half the time. Fact is, small teams are nimbler and can change direction and shift focus in ways that would bring most larger teams to a standstill. They are also free to experiment with design ideas that may be better suited for limited usage. You can see that ethos in Mercedes-AMG today. If you look across the AMG line over the last few years, you'll see several preposterous but amazing vehicles: a 2.5-ton rigid axle SUV with a 6.0 Liter Biturbo V-12 and *enough traction to climb Mt. Everest.* (Translation for the less car-savvy: It produces more power than three modern-day Honda Accords combined.) Or you can choose a station wagon that serves as the official medical car for the Formula 1 racing. Keep in mind these are extremely low-volume production vehicles. Just imagine the challenge they would present for a large-scale automaker, even one with the resources that Mercedes has.

Homegrown Talent

There is no doubt that a few engineers who work for Daimler are living out their lifelong dreams. Working for the brand that developed the first automobile and having your ideas make it into production is a big deal that puts you in rare company. But what happens when those who are tasked with leading the team don't have the same enthusiasm, the same desire to break new ground? Does this have a tangible impact on the team, especially if that decision-maker didn't come from the ranks of the team? Oftentimes, the answer will be yes. Unfortunately, with most large organizations, the decision-makers will join the team from the outside. There are cases where bringing in outside talent will be unavoidable, I will admit. However, their lack of experience with the team can lead to a less-than-desirable team chemistry. Their inability to understand what *really* makes the team click can become a key liability if the team fails to execute at a critical time.

By comparison, with a smaller team, you can almost guarantee that those leading the group have come from within their ranks. They know the work at the same level as the junior team members and can jump in and help if necessary. What this does for team chemistry is immeasurable. To know that your management team has experienced the same frustrations, hurdles, and setbacks as you can only instill confidence. You know the advice they offer is meant to move the process forward in a genuine fashion, not simply make a report look good. Credibility is never an issue. Remember, even after its first twenty or so years AMG's team was no bigger than roughly a hundred employees. By the time AMG was acquired by Daimler, this team had worked together very closely for a long time. They shared numerous accomplishments as a team, so their merger into the larger Daimler umbrella didn't affect their work. AMG was still AMG. And it has remained this way ever since.

* * *

Arch Motorcycles

The impact of a product can be measured by its ability to influence the world around it. Traditional logic suggests that the greater the impact of something, the larger the company that produced it. Conversely, smaller companies have a smaller impact. When you look back to the glory days of manufacturing, you see this logic laid out in its full glory. For many companies, their dominance in a sector was based on their size.

General Motors in the '80s and '90s is a great example: With at least six brands under one corporate umbrella and multiple versions of the same vehicle on sale against each other, it was easy for GM to be seen as an automotive juggernaut. That size, however, did not save GM during the downturn that occurred in 2008–2009. Instead, it highlighted what I believe to be a flaw in the bigger-is-better theory. Is it possible to grow so large that you dilute the cachet of your product or service? Is bigger really better if you begin sacrificing quality to meet quantitative benchmarks?

Technology has allowed larger companies to shrink their overall footprint without losing their position in the marketplace. And smaller companies are now able to project themselves onto the world stage without having a physical presence in London, NYC, Hong Kong, or Abu Dhabi. The current trend for smaller teams in a company's formative stages doesn't appear to be reversing either. So clearly there are times when the size of the company does *not* correlate with the impact of its products, despite historical trends. In fact, when we see this formula reversed and a product's impact is far larger than the company that produced it, we tend to see that as a positive, of someone punching above their weight.

A recent example of this "small company, big impact" dynamic comes to us courtesy of the motorcycle world. When it comes to modern-day motorcycle riders, anyone willing to strap themselves to two wheels with speeds of more than 100 mph is going to be a tough audience. Which means if you're going to stand out in this crowd, playing it safe ain't going to cut it. You're going to need something genuinely special to hold the attention of this bunch. How does a new company establish itself in a market filled with names like Harley-Davidson, Indian, Ducati, and Buell? You keep it small. You keep it powerful. And you keep it unique.

Arch Motorcycles is a fascinating example of this process. It's an example of what happens when people who care about their product and their consumer equally come together to build a company. It doesn't hurt to have a legitimate Hollywood action hero, Keanu Reeves (who's known for being an avid rider), as part of the founding team. For many potential buyers that would be enough, but Arch's customers get another bonus in the form of Gard Hollinger, the highly respected bike builder from Los Angeles. Very much like the team behind AMG, at Arch you've got true believers who are ready to place quality over quantity. They're searching for something exact, something exclusive—a feeling you get from only *their* bikes.

The genesis of this partnership was based on the tiniest of requests (albeit a unique one). It all started when Reeves visited Hollinger in 2007 about making a modification to his bike:

Reeves: Can you build me a sissy bar?

Hollinger: We don't build sissy bars.

Reeves: Oh, then what do you do?

Hollinger: We make motorcycles.

Reeves: Well . . . are you interested in making a motorcycle?

Hollinger: I don't know, what sort of motorcycle do you wanna make?[21]

47

Hollinger didn't add a sissy bar (a slang term for a support rest at the back of a bike seat) to Reeves's bike. Instead, he created a one-off cycle for Reeves that would later serve as the foundation on which the nascent company would eventually be built on. It would take several attempts before Reeves was able to convince Hollinger that a business model existed and was worth pursuing.

"It was really riding the prototype that was the proof of the business concept, even though we didn't know it," Reeves told *Bloomberg* in a 2016 story about the company. "It was this idea of a big V-twin, a long wheel base with modern grade suspension and the telemetry that Gard had designed and the ergonomics. It was this package that I wanted from the first time riding that bike. I'd never ridden anything like that. . . . I told him, 'OK, the reason we should do this is because the machine is amazing, and we're going to die' [anyway]. Let's make something."[22]

And that they did. It took awhile before they moved from prototype to a finished product, but the product was everything you want when you're looking to introduce yourself to the world. Its official name was the KRGT-1 and that bike debuted in 2014. Each bike is custom built by a team of roughly a dozen people, and contains nearly two hundred individual, hand-made parts. The gas tank alone requires sixty-plus hours of carving billet metal before it can be fitted to the bike. The bikes are so customized that each owner participates in "fitting sessions" to ensure that the

---

[21] https://newatlas.com/keanu-reeves-arch-motorcycle-company-krgt-1/34360

[22] https://www.bloomberg.com/news/articles/2016-08-15/keanu-reeves-will-build-a-78-000-arch-motorcycle-just-for-you

pedals, handlebars, and seat angle are tailored to their comfort. After that, each bike gets a shakedown ride by Keanu himself to confirm everything is as it should be. This is the world of bespoke bike building at its best. For all of this, the total wait time for a bike is just shy of three months.[23]

While actual production numbers are a bit of a secret, the many Arch bikes out there in the wild have been received with nothing but praise. Read through professional reviews and you'll notice the accolades pile up rather quickly. With just a single bike in its lineup to begin with, and Keanu as part of the team, Arch could have been seen as a one-trick pony. If you're only going to make one bike, how hard could it be to do right? In 2017, though, Arch answered its critics with the introduction of two additional models, the 1S and the Method 143, extending their product line to a grand total of three bikes. In doing so, they went from boutique manufacturer to legitimate bike builders. None of what made the original product unique was lost in these new offerings. The construction process remained the same at the small offices where the KRGT-1 was born. The high levels of craftsmanship were retained, and Reeves is still riding the bikes to ensure "you get the giggles when you ride them."[24]

The future of Arch is unknown, but all indicators point toward a healthy future. Imaginative products, a rabid client base, and an unwavering desire to deliver a

[23] Ibid

[24] Ibid

specific experience are the components you want to see in any organization. What's behind this winning recipe?

Sometimes It's What You Can't See that Matters

As I noted earlier, the first bike, which started in 2007, turned out to be a prototype. It allowed Reeves and Hollinger to work through their design and engineering philosophy. They didn't move into major production until late 2014—that is, six to seven years after building the prototype. Over such a long time period, the natural inclination to keep up with prevailing industry trends could have easily overwhelmed them and pushed their product in a direction completely different than the one they initially gravitated toward. Can you imagine the difficulty you'd face in keeping a team focused on a single product for that length of time?

Parkinson's Law of Triviality comes to mind here. Developed by British historian Cyril Northcote Parkinson, in its simplest form it's an observation about the human tendency to devote a great deal of time to unimportant details while crucial matters go unattended to. In some circles it's known as "bike shedding," a reference to Parkinson's observation of a committee that had been organized to approve plans for a nuclear power plant. As Parkinson noted, the committee devoted a disproportionate amount of time to relatively unimportant details—such as the materials for a bicycle storage shed—which limited the time available to focus on the design of the nuclear plant.[25]

---

[25] https://whatis.techtarget.com/definition/Parkinsons-law-of-triviality-bikeshedding

Now apply that concept to a scenario where your first product takes upwards of six years to design, develop, and test. Imagine how easy it would be to get hung up on details that pull you away from the core product. Keeping any team focused over long stretches of time is a challenge, but it's clear that these bikes were being built to a very specific standard from the outset. Unlike more mass-produced motorcycles, which target a broader demographic, these bikes were aiming to be a sensation—a unique experience that a select group of riders would understand and appreciate. (And it would come from an $80,000 purchase, remember, so we aren't talking pocket change.) Remaining true to your vision is a difficult undertaking under the best of circumstances; just consider what happens each time a new individual is added to the mix. You run the risk of having the original vision diluted with new ideas and input that pulls you away from the original outline.

Simply put, you need a team that's dedicated more to the team goal then they are to their own personal ambitions, a team that realizes everyone's success is interconnected. Smaller teams make progress toward a common vision easier to monitor from within. As the team inevitably grows, however, you will have situations where newer team members are disconnected from the genesis of the mission. That distance can manifest itself in feelings of being ignored, which results in decreased motivation and potentially lower effort all the way around. If your team is small enough and close enough you can check in with members personally at regular intervals. Your personal involvement lets the team know that they aren't out on the island by themselves, and you can work to reinforce the purpose behind the original vision while providing opportunities for team members to provide input into that vision.

Harvey Specter

Now as much as I have argued that small teams can be the key to success, don't be fooled—size still matters. Large organizations still have the benefit of perception. Most people will look at a larger organization and assume they have their shit together. If they didn't, they probably wouldn't have grown so big. As an example, Harley-Davidson has roughly four hundred dealers in the US, and they sell millions of dollars in merchandise alone. For about a decade, Ford Motor Company even sold a Harley-Davidson branded F-150. That's presence. Considering how easy it is for the average person to equate Harley-Davidson with motorcycles in general, they are in the enviable position of not having to break new barriers with their marketing and promotion. Their branding doesn't have to be the most memorable or creative. It needs to be consistent— a reminder that they're ready for you when the time is right. After you've seen them everywhere, you're likely to consider them the default motorcycle choice purely from the overwhelming exposure.

Arch, and other companies in their position, don't have the luxury of such massive name recognition. So if they want to get noticed they have to take a different course of action. And that they have. Their approach brings to mind a quote from Harvey Specter, a character on the USA network show *Suits*. Played by the actor Gabriel

Macht, he is a brash lawyer who is keen on winning. Among his many quotable lines from the show, I think the following is apropos when it comes to our current discussion: *"Win a no-win situation by rewriting the rules."*

In contrast to Harley-Davidson, Arch is smaller and doesn't have the same brand cachet. So, they started rewriting the rules. They've been far more strategic with their marketing, and that's where they've been able to leverage what makes them different. If the goal is to make consumers aware of their brand, how about a Neiman Marcus and Arch Motorcycles-inspired riding experience? The wealthy few who can afford this get two days of riding with Reeves and Hollinger through the Santa Monica mountains and Angeles National Forest. It'll set you back $150K, but I don't think you'll get that kind of opportunity at your local motorcycle franchise dealer.[26] Throw in a Super Bowl commercial for the website builder Squarespace that includes Reeves standing on top of a moving Arch motorcycle, and I think you can begin to see the point.[27]

Arch is flexing its muscles the only way an upstart business can: by looking at the box and deciding it's more effective to stay on the outside. Smaller teams tend to have more leeway when it comes to being rebellious. We expect quirky and unpredictable things

---

[26] https://www.hotcars.com/why-is-everyone-talking-about-keanu-reeves-motorcycle-company/

[27] https://www.rideapart.com/articles/245086/keanus-not-so-death-defying-super-bowl-ad/

from them because we understand they're looking to make a big impression. The business world is peppered with stories of big companies being outflanked by smaller companies with guerilla business strategies. Airbnb and Dollar Shave Club immediately come to mind. Smaller teams should be able to coalesce around this concept and form in such a way that maximizes attitude, vision, speed, and distinctiveness.

Truth III

Special Operations Forces (SOF) cannot be mass-produced.

{Elite teams are not like microwave ready meals}

"I was an overnight success all right, but thirty years is a long, long night." - Ray Kroc

Let's get this out of the way: There is no such thing as an overnight success. No one we consider to be great did anything overnight. The term is a misnomer and I say we chuck it, permanently. When we think of successful teams what we actually see is the culmination of days, weeks, and years of working together. Whether it be a soul-stirring live music performance or a dominating sports feat, the accomplishments we marvel at are typically second nature for the people who achieve them. This is why the term "overnight success" is so imprecise. It's the easiest way for those of us on the outside to describe success that appeared with no advance notice or introduction. *We didn't see it coming, so it had to be overnight.*

No matter what arena of life you consider, the teams we place highest on the pedestal make everything seem easy. Earth, Wind & Fire. The Apollo 11 crew. Carol Burnett and Friends. Bill Russell's Celtics. For many of us, these unique groupings exemplify greatness with such ease your only option is to admire it. They make everything look so damn easy.

While we're truth-telling here, let's be clear about something else: You don't reach the level of teamwork and effectiveness required to *land on the moon* without a key ingredient: *patience.* This is where many first-time leaders will end up dropping the ball. And truthfully, so will a good number of mid-to-senior-level ones. They will respond to the pressures of business by rushing their teams and attempting to accelerate their learning curves in hopes of showing production value as early as possible. The problem with this light-speed method is that it makes it more difficult for a company to retain new hires, hardly an effective long-term strategy.

A 2014 survey commissioned by BambooHR, a human resources software company, offers several nuggets of wisdom on the topic of onboarding. According to its findings:

- 16.45 percent of respondents left a new job within their first week of employment, and 31 percent left within the first six months.
- New hires with entry-level or intermediate-level roles are the most likely to leave a company; they represent 43 percent and 38 percent of a company's exodus, respectively.
- 45 percent of HR personnel surveyed reported that ineffective onboarding will cost companies upwards of $10,000 a year in wasted money.

As you can see, for many firms it's an uphill battle just keeping the people they hired. And the actual costs of this light speed method are evident, even to the HR staff. If you can't keep the staff you've taken on, you certainly won't be able to shorten the time between the hiring phase and productivity phase. And given the evolving nature of the American workforce and the accompanying skills gap, the need for more technically skilled labor is set to be a big challenge. How many companies will be able to keep pace? With current trends, it's as if employees are being viewed as short-term bets instead of long-term investments. Logic would dictate that a properly trained employee is going to be far more productive in the long run. It's too bad so many management teams are missing this point.

There are a number of professional sports teams I could have used as an illustrative example of my argument. But to really get the point across, I had to genuinely take some time and consider who in our modern-day business world has had a run that would rival the most consistently successful sports franchise.

* * *

The Oracle of Omaha

Warren Buffet. Berkshire Hathaway. These names are synonymous with long-term success. Buffet is the businessman that businessmen look up to. Berkshire Hathaway is a global conglomerate with a stock price so high you rarely even see the stock traded. As of the writing of this book (Q2 of 2019), a single share of Class A stock is valued at $297,060.00. For many of us, it can be hard to quantify just how successful Buffet and Berkshire really are. So let's run through some basics about them:

- In 1982 *Forbes* printed their first list of the richest four hundred Americans. Buffet was on the list and has been every year since. His personal wealth at the time was reported to be $250 million.
- In 1965 he purchased the controlling shares of Berkshire Hathaway stock for something in the neighborhood of $11 per share.
- In 1983 the stock rose to roughly $1,000 a share. (As a point of comparison, note how excited everyone got when Apple hit $1,000 a share—thirty years later.)

- In 1996 a single share of Berkshire peaked at $30,000.
- Ten years later, Berkshire stock ballooned to $100,000 per share.
- By 2016, Berkshire shares hit the almost-unimaginable mark of $250,000 per share, and have remained at that level or higher ever since.[28]

The return on that original $11 investment is far too great for me to attempt to calculate, but it's safe to say it's significant enough that had you been able to invest alongside Buffet even in the '80s, you would be ultra-wealthy right now. And this was accomplished without any shortcuts or gimmicks. Fortunately for those who work directly for Berkshire and their subsidiaries, Buffet's management philosophy is also free of gimmickry. Early on he decided to run his companies with a unique set of values, and he has remained true to them to this day. In a business world where management teams and corporate boards love to dive into new management trends, Buffet stays the course. The genesis of this philosophy can be seen in this 1979 letter to shareholders:

Berkshire is run on the principle of centralization of financial decisions at the top (the very top, it might be added), and rather extreme delegation of operating authority to a number of key managers at the individual company or business unit level. We could just field a

---

[28] https://www.fool.com/investing/2017/06/01/5-key-moments-in-berkshire-hathaway-stock-history.aspx

basketball team with our corporate headquarters group.

This approach produces an occasional major mistake that might have been eliminated or minimized through closer operating controls. But it also eliminates large layers of costs and dramatically speeds decision-making. Because everyone has a great deal to do, a very great deal gets done. Most important of all, it enables us to attract and retain some extraordinarily talented individuals—people who simply can't be hired in the normal course of events—who find working for Berkshire to be almost identical to running their own show.

We have placed much trust in them—and their achievements have far exceeded that trust.[29]

Some forty years later there's been little change in the way Berkshire operates. At the business unit level or individual company level operational decisions are still handled by the respective leadership teams. This level of trust instills in those decision-makers the autonomy and sense of ownership necessary to guide their divisions. With decision-making pushed downward, Buffett and his team are free to plot the trajectory of the overall company. Buffet may not be the only oracle in Omaha, either. If you've followed his ascension into the pantheon of ultra-successful businessman, then you'll also know the name Charlie Munger. Munger, vice chairman of Berkshire Hathaway, has been working

---

[29] http://masonmyers.com/berkshire-hathaway-management-structure/

alongside Buffet since 1978. For some historical perspective, here's what was going on the year they joined forces:

- The S&P 500 index opened that year at $90.25 a share.[30]
- The Nasdaq stock exchange was only seven years old, having been formed in 1971.
- Coca Cola finished the year with a share price of $0.91.[31]

That's a long time to work together. In that spirit, I'm going to issue you a little challenge: Look around your own organization and identify at least three people who have forty years of continuous service. At first blush, this might not be that difficult. But, to increase the level of difficulty, I'm going to need at least one of these folks to occupy a senior-level position, something akin to vice chairman. You'll be hard-pressed to find such a person, I'd be willing to bet. Buffet and Munger have known each other personally for upwards of sixty years since being introduced by a mutual friend. "We went to dinner and in five minutes, Charlie was rolling on the floor laughing at his own jokes—and I do the same thing," Buffet recalled in a recent interview.[32]

Their relationship is based on an unusually high level of mutual regard. It's been reported that they've never

[30] https://www.multpl.com/s-p-500-historical-prices/table/by-year

[31] https://www.macrotrends.net/stocks/charts/KO/coca-cola/stock-price-history

[32] https://www.cnbc.com/2019/01/31/warren-buffett-on-his-successful-relationship-with-charlie-munger.html

argued with each other after forty years of working together. Obviously, their relationship is unique, but that's what makes it work. Two men who would've likely been extraordinarily successful on their own have managed to coexist in a business world that lives under the mantra "What have you done for me lately?" The payoff from forty years of being colleagues and sixty years of friendship is unique as well, as Berkshire currently manages more than $736 billion in assets. Add to that the fact that the company has outperformed the overall stock market every year since 1960, and this argument begins to speak for itself.[33]

In case you take this to be a singular example of senior-level longevity within Berkshire, I assure you it isn't. Greg Abel, the chairman and CEO of Berkshire's energy division, and Ajit Jain, vice chair of insurance operations, have both been with the company for at least twenty-five years each. By some accounts, these are the men who will lead Berkshire into the future.[34]

Which brings me to the heart of my argument. The most elite teams cannot be thrown together haphazardly and expected to be effective, much less successful. If there is one constant throughout this discussion, it's patience. Buffet sees time as an opportunity, not an obligation. Many of you will simply see Berkshire as a reminder of how corporate America became what it is. Two guys with the right connections were fortunate enough to

---

[33] Ibid.

[34] https://fortune.com/2018/05/07/warren-buffett-four-successors

make the right investments early and just sit on them. What's so outstanding about that you might ask?

I can hear many of you saying, today's business world moves too fast for this to be a winning recipe any longer. Product life cycles have been halved, translating into an increased pace of development and deployment. Organizations need to see a return on their investment in employees at a faster pace. On top of that, no one thinks about working for the same company for anywhere near forty years. And a cursory glance at employee tenure data supports that latter point. According to the Bureau of Labor Statistics, in January 2018 the median number of years that wage and salary workers had been with their current employer was 4.2 years, a figure unchanged from January 2016.[35]

But there's a question that should follow that data: why? What's happened that makes such a large portion of the workforce want to get on the move after only five years? Is it a continuation of the trend we discussed earlier in the chapter, where more employees are apt to change jobs even if it's in the first six months? Is it a case of employees recognizing the minimal investments into their careers, while the employers simultaneously look to maximize return on their skills? It's a fascinating question and one we can explore in more detail at a later time. Suffice to say, the result is fewer employees who are prepared to commit long term. Which presents a dilemma? Do you jump on board the prevailing trend

---

[35] https://www.bls.gov/news.release/tenure.nr0.htm

of "not now, but right now"? Or do you pick your team, give em' some space and wait?

Habituation

I'm going to share a personal story here. I, like roughly 10 percent of the world's population, am left-handed. The oddball out when it came to scissors, notebooks, and elementary school desks. But when it comes to sports, I have an advantage. Growing up I played basketball regularly. I was far from a superstar, but my left-handedness offered opportunity. On the surface this state of affairs may not seem like much, but statistically it meant there was a good chance I was the only left-hander on the court, which mattered. Left-handed basketball players can present a problem because most people don't play against them frequently enough to learn how to defend them.

Everything about their game is the exact opposite of what you instinctively want to do. One of my friends from middle school realized this and was quick to point it out. We played ball together over the course of high school and college and whenever we hit the court, he would look at me and say, "They ain't ready." To opposing players, this may have come across as the typical back-and-forth you hear on every basketball court. What he actually meant was they weren't expecting a left-handed player, so take advantage of it for as long as you can.

The more we played, the more in sync we became. He could see a matchup that favored me and be ready to exploit it at a moment's notice. No matter where we played, we knew how our game was going to go. I share this anecdote in hopes of helping you see how time invested between collaborators can lead to familiarity, and familiarity can bring a level of composure that allows for consistent performances even under unknown circumstances. Now, I don't expect you to use my recreational basketball legacy as a building block for what you do with the team in your office (even if it does give me a chance to recognize a good friend in print). So let's see what professional researchers have to say about the topic.

In a group of studies helmed by Harvard Business School professor Robert S. Huckman and University of North Carolina professor Bradley Staats in 2013, the effects of familiarity between teams were analyzed in multiple workplaces. The results should not be ignored:

- At a software services firm, a 50 percent increase in team familiarity was followed by a 19 percent decrease in product defects and a 30 percent decrease in budgetary deviations.
- In audit and consulting teams that were studied, high familiarity yielded a 10 percent improvement in performance as judged by clients.[36]

In a different study, from 2006, Huckman and fellow Harvard Business School professor Gary Pisano measured the success rate of two hundred cardiac surgeons from forty-three different hospitals to determine whether having star performers or an

---

[36] https://hbr.org/2013/12/the-hidden-benefits-of-keeping-teams-intact.

effective team led to better outcomes. Again, I'd ask you to seriously consider the findings:

After analyzing more than 38,000 procedures, Huckman and Pisano found that the performance of individual heart specialists did improve significantly with practice and experience—but only at the hospitals where they did most of their work. When the same surgeons left their usual teams to work at different hospitals, their success rates returned to baseline. The study suggests that working within a bonded team of colleagues helps develop interactive routines that harness the unique talents of each team member.[37] One more thing: The researchers concluded that elite performance is not as portable as previously thought. In reality, it is more a function of the "familiarity that a surgeon develops with the assets of a given organization."[38]

When do you remember being able to report to your senior-level managers that you'd found a way to decrease mistakes or defects by 20 percent, and without some sort of sleight of hand? Or being able to report your budget with 30 percent more accuracy because of a decrease in deviations? Simply put, when teams are more familiar with each other, the likelihood that they will be able to perform in a consistent manner increases.

Project Aristotle

---

[37] https://positivepsychologyprogram.com/psychology-teamwork.

[38] Ibid.

When members of a team have a strong familiarity with each other, it's only natural for them to become more confident as a unit. In turn, increased confidence will lead to increased performance and a more effective team. For these reasons the brains over at Google have spent quite a bit of time researching the factors that make for an effective team. Project Aristotle, as a recent company initiative was titled, took a deep look at 180 teams within the Google family. The teams included a mix of performance levels, so as not to only include the best of the best and end up with one-sided results.[39]

The study identified five variables that had an impact on team success: psychological safety, dependability, structure and clarity, meaning, and impact. The most important one was found to be psychological safety, which researchers define as "a belief that a team is safe for risk taking in the face of being seen as ignorant, incompetent, negative, or disruptive."

"In a team with high psychological safety, teammates feel safe to take risks around their team members," the study asserted. "They feel confident that no one on the team will embarrass or punish anyone else for admitting a mistake, asking a question, or offering a new idea."[40] Researchers found that individuals who report being on teams with higher psychological safety are:

- less likely to leave the company

---

[39] https://rework.withgoogle.com/print/guides/5721312655835136/

[40] Ibid.

- more likely to harness the power of diverse ideas
- more likely to generate more revenue for the company
- rated "effective" by executives twice as often as individuals not reporting higher psychological safety

Now it may be possible that at some point Buffet came across studies offering similar information and applied their message. But whether he did or not, the fact is since 1979 he's provided the men and women who run the companies that make up Berkshire the space to make their own decisions. You could argue that he's been fostering "psychological safety" for years, and everyone else is just now catching up to him.

In keeping with the Berkshire theme of this chapter, we'll look at how these factors apply specifically to Berkshire companies. In 2015 Stanford Business School professors David Larcker and Brian Tayan conducted a survey with roughly eighty CEOs of Berkshire Hathaway subsidiaries. The executives, who worked in a variety of industries, had an average tenure of twelve years. The levels of autonomy they report might be refreshingly surprising to those of us outside of Berkshire. For them, acting on their authority is to be expected:

- Berkshire Hathaway operating managers . . . believe that ownership by Berkshire allows them to manage their businesses with a longer performance horizon than would be the case under different ownership. Respondents vary in terms of what performance horizon they use to manage their companies, with the average being 12 years.

This compares with an estimated 1- to 3-year performance horizon if their business were owned by another company.

- All respondents have identified at least one successor as CEO. . . . They convey their views on succession to Mr. Buffett, including their primary recommendation for a successor, other potential successors, and the strengths and weaknesses of candidates. (By comparison, only half [51 percent] of public and private companies claim to have identified a permanent successor to the current CEO.)[41]

- What's more, these managers also report that their communication with Buffet is allowed to happen on *their* schedule. They do not operate under a regimen that defines when they should reach out to him nor how many times a year they should make contact. For what it's worth, the title of this report is "Trust and Consequences."

I could continue to bombard you with all types of stats that show how hugely successful Berkshire is as an entity. And much of it undeniably stems from Buffet's long-term, stick-to-the-fundamentals type of approach. But I hope you get the point: There is very little that will replace the overwhelming benefits of building a team, giving them the proper space and tools to grow, and doing everything within your power to encourage their work over as many years as possible. A strategy that is shockingly simple yet effective.

---

[41] https://papers.ssrn.com/sol3/papers.cfm?abstract_id=2678556, p. 2

I'll close this section out with a few words from the big man himself: "We give each [manager] a simple mission: Just run your business as if: 1) you own 100 percent of it; 2) it is the only asset in the world that you and your family have or will ever have and 3) you can't sell or merge it for at least a century."[42] When you can see your employees through this type of lens, you will have become the leader you've dreamed about being.

---

[42] https://papers.ssrn.com/sol3/papers.cfm?abstract_id=2678556, p. 1

Truth IV

Competent Special Operations Forces cannot be created after emergencies occur.
{Competent teams cannot be created after emergencies occur}

"It wasn't raining when Noah built the Ark."

- Howard Ruff

Planning and preparation are essential to any task, whether it's climbing Mt. Everest, launching a new product line, or baking sugar cookies. The presence of these two components are what separate those who are calm in the eye of the storm from those who run around like a chicken with its head cut off. I'm sure many of you are familiar with the saying "Practice makes perfect"; I prefer to think of it as "Practice makes permanence." And permanence is exactly what you want when the situation around you begins deteriorating. If you doubt this, consider the following questions: What happens when your team isn't fully prepared for the eventual emergencies that will occur? How will their response reflect on you as the leader? Will it have a lasting effect on your team's overall confidence?

At some point, we've all planned for bad weather. If you're in a region where winters are long and harsh, you keep plenty of firewood stocked up, and potentially a generator for long-term power outages. For those of you who live in dry regions of the country, rain barrels and other methods of conserving water are used to address the water shortages that inevitably happen. And if you live near the coastline, hurricane-rated storm shutters are just as important. So it stands to reason that if we as individuals must prepare for the worst, our federal agencies should be prepared in the same way. At least you'd think so.

* * *

Hurricane Katrina

On August 29, 2005, Hurricane Katrina made landfall on the Gulf Coast of the United States as a Category-3 storm with sustained winds of 100–140 mph. The storm covered an area of land 400 miles across. It began as a depression over the Bahamas on August 23, and by all accounts all the normal warnings were issued. As August 28 approached the evacuation process began across the entire region. On that day, the National Weather Service made the following prediction: "Most of the [Gulf Coast] area will be uninhabitable for weeks . .. perhaps longer."[43]

At particular risk was New Orleans, a city steeped in music, food, and dance—a true melting pot of cultures. New Orleans is a municipality with topographical challenges, with Lake Pontchartrain to the north and the mighty Mississippi bordering it to the east and west. Not to mention, roughly half the city sits six feet below sea level. Because of its precarious location, networks of levees and seawalls have been put into place to prevent or minimize flooding into the city. As everyone would soon come to learn, however, the supposed safeguards on the eastern and western borders of the city were far less reliable than expected.

On August 28, Mayor Ray Nagin issued a city-wide evacuation order in an attempt to get people out of the

---

[43] History.com Staff. "Hurricane Katrina." History.com, A&E Television Networks, 2009, www.history.com/topics/hurricane-katrina.

path of the storm and any potential follow-up flooding. At that time New Orleans had a population of roughly 500,000 people, so an evacuation of that magnitude was a challenge by any stretch of the imagination. It was complicated further by the fact that nearly a quarter of those residents didn't have access to a vehicle.[44] The mayor designated the Superdome, the home of the New Orleans Saints, as a shelter of last resort, because it was located downtown and on ground higher than most other parts of the city. The arena would see roughly 10,000 people show up for shelter in the first few hours of the storm. 80 percent of the city did manage to evacuate, while a large number of the city's remaining residents chose to wait out the storm in their homes.

When August 29 arrived, the storm surge peaked as high as twenty-seven feet in some locations. For comparison, we're talking about the height of a typical two-story structure. Preceding the surge were several hours of heavy rain across an area that covered three states at its widest band. All of which meant New Orleans had no chance of escaping the water. Introduce hours of heavy rain accompanied by one-hundred-plus mph winds to a city that sits partially below sea level, and you have all the ingredients for a massive weather-related catastrophe. By 9 a.m. on August 29, residents who remained behind were already making their way to rooftops and attics to avoid the rising waters. New Orleans would sacrifice nearly 80 percent of the city to Katrina in water-related damage.

---

[44] Ibid.

By all estimates Katrina was the first disaster to come near the hundred-billion-dollar mark, making it one of if not the most expensive natural disasters to ever occur in the continental United States. Here's the data:

Housing	$67 billion
Consumer durable goods	$7 billion
Business property	$20 billion
Government property	$3 billion
Total	**$96 billion**

Table 1.1 Estimate damage from Hurricane Katrina and the New Orleans Flood[45]

And these are just some of the statistics. Over 2.5 million customers reported power outages in Louisiana, Mississippi, and Alabama. Thirty-eight emergency (911) call centers were taken offline along with three million phone lines in the same three states. The commercial broadcast sector wasn't spared either: 44 percent of TV stations went off the air and 50 percent of area radio stations went down as well.[46] You had citizens without power, water, food, or information. Homes were severely wind damaged or flooded outright. Local municipalities weren't capable of responding for the

---

[45] United States, Congress, "The Federal Response to Hurricane Katrina: Lessons Learned, February 2006." The Federal Response to Hurricane Katrina: Lessons Learned, February 2006, Government Printing Office, 2006, p.7

[46] United States, Congress, "The Federal Response to Hurricane Katrina: Lessons Learned, February 2006." The Federal Response to Hurricane Katrina: Lessons Learned, February 2006, Government Printing Office, 2006, p.8

same reasons, and virtually no one was able to communicate on a local level during the crisis. These are the type of circumstances where the federal government is supposed to step in with its resources and knowledge.

To fully understand the federal government's reaction to Hurricane Katrina, I recommend reading *The Federal Response to Hurricane Katrina: Lessons Learned.* Published in February 2006, it is a 228-page report commissioned by the Bush administration that walks through everything that happened before, during, and after the storm in detail. To summarize things for the purposes of this discussion: The feds dropped the ball. Here's how.

When it comes to disaster response in the US, help begins at the local (city) level. The cities have resources and personnel available to address their weather-related disasters. But if they expend all their resources or show that they have been rendered useless, they can request assistance from the state. The state, in turn, must follow a similar path, but with an additional wrinkle: Nearby states, who will typically bring additional resources to bear under mutual aid agreements, are called on next. These agreements are in place to provide regional support for neighboring states. If the storm damage had been limited to Louisiana only, Alabama and Mississippi could have pitched in. Or vice versa. Unfortunately, with Katrina, that wasn't the case. All three states were slammed.

When a state has exhausted its resources, and neighboring states can't answer the call for help, the state turns to the federal government for additional assistance. Reporting shows that all the necessary city, state, and federal disaster declarations were made in advance for Katrina. Which meant that no one should have had to wait for the storm to hit before personnel, funding, and other necessary resources were authorized. Supplies and staff were pre-positioned prior to the storm, and there was daily communication with the White House beginning a few days prior to the storm.[47]

Despite all these precautions and warnings, however, the actual response would fall incredibly short of effective. Descriptions of the damage following Katrina's touchdown are best left to those who were responsible for restoring the region back to its pre-Katrina state:

"I can only imagine that this is what Hiroshima looked like sixty years ago."

—Haley Barbour, Mississippi governor

"The Port of Gulfport, Mississippi, was left with virtually nothing and must rebuild almost from scratch." —Norman Mineta, Secretary of Transportation

"The magnitude of the storm was such that the local communications system wasn't simply degraded, it was, at least for a period of time, destroyed."

—Paul McHale, Assistant Secretary of Defense for Homeland Defense[48]

---

[47] United States, Congress, "The Federal Response to Hurricane Katrina: Lessons Learned, February 2006." The Federal Response to Hurricane Katrina: Lessons Learned, February 2006, Government Printing Office, 2006, p. 14

[48] United States, Congress, "The Federal Response to Hurricane Katrina: Lessons Learned, February 2006." The Federal Response to Hurricane Katrina: Lessons Learned, February 2006, Government Printing Office, 2006, p. 34

In many people's eyes New Orleans would become the epicenter of post-storm dysfunction. For several days following the storm, Mayor Nagin operated out of a hotel near the Superdome with no reliable or continuous communication with the world outside. The superintendent of the New Orleans Police Department later confirmed to Congress that approximately 147 officers had abandoned their posts. Trapped residents who weren't able to escape the rising waters were swept away, their bodies floating in the still waters of New Orleans as the storm receded.[49] Local damage assessments regarding the levees was complicated by confusion over the type of damage that had occurred throughout the system. On top of this, because of glitches in communication infrastructure officials were forced to rely on a patchwork of private, commercial, and governmental lines. Anyone could see that under these circumstances it was nearly impossible to lay out a plan to make repairs and get the city back on track.

Back at the Superdome, the refuge of last resort, a small catastrophe in its own right was unrolling. Prior to the storm, as part of the early preparation process, FEMA had staged nearly 44,000 MREs (Meals Ready to Eat) and 90,000 liters of water at the Superdome for onsite evacuees.[50] The National Guard provided roughly six hundred soldiers to operate in a law enforcement and

[49] United States, Congress, "The Federal Response to Hurricane Katrina: Lessons Learned, February 2006." The Federal Response to Hurricane Katrina: Lessons Learned, February 2006, Government Printing Office, 2006, p. 37

[50] United States, Congress, "The Federal Response to Hurricane Katrina: Lessons Learned, February 2006." The Federal Response to Hurricane Katrina: Lessons Learned, February 2006, Government Printing Office, 2006, p. 29

security role as well. They were joined by a contingent of medical personnel which included five physicians, four nurses, and twenty medics.[51] All of this proved to be woefully inadequate, and conditions inside the arena deteriorated rapidly.

Though actual reports vary it's estimated that some twenty thousand people would ultimately be evacuated from the Superdome after the storm passed. Because it had been identified in the city's disaster response plan as the primary evacuation zone, most people seeking evacuation from the city had migrated to it. This number of arrivals exceeded the original estimates for that location and started a chain reaction of events that only added to the confusion, hysteria, and panic. This would become a recurring theme throughout the days following Katrina.

The convention center, which had not been designated as a shelter or evacuation point, evolved into an unofficial central location for evacuees because of its location on higher ground. Estimates would later put some 25,000 people there, leading to yet another slow-moving catastrophe. Unlike at the Superdome, no supplies had been pre-staged there, so those fortunate enough to be rescued but unfortunate enough to be dropped at the convention center would have a whole new set of issues waiting for them. Those issues would play out live and nearly nonstop in front of the world over the following few days.

[51] United States, Congress, "The Federal Response to Hurricane Katrina: Lessons Learned, February 2006." The Federal Response to Hurricane Katrina: Lessons Learned, February 2006, Government Printing Office, 2006, p. 30

It is impossible in this chapter—or even this book—to recount all the breakdowns that occurred throughout the region and inside New Orleans specifically. In essence, the entire command and control structure for New Orleans and the states of Louisiana, Alabama, and Mississippi had been washed away in the storm. The after-action report prepared for President Bush highlighted three areas that shaped the (lack of) federal response. I'll quote the report directly:

- First, the sheer amount of destruction over such a large area created an enormous demand for emergency assistance such as fuel, medical supplies, food, shelter, and water. This demand, coupled with the austere conditions throughout the Gulf Coast following Katrina's landfall, exceeded FEMA's standard disaster delivery capabilities and processes.

- Second, localities needed assistance to perform emergency response operations and reestablish incident command. However, Hurricane Katrina's impact across the Gulf Coast region limited the use of normal mutual aid agreements, which rely on neighboring cities and counties for assistance. In this case, the neighboring jurisdictions were overwhelmed themselves and unable to aid elsewhere. Assistance had to come from states outside the region and from the federal government. This requirement for an active federal role in emergency response operations was most pronounced in New Orleans.

- Finally, the communications problems had a debilitating effect on response efforts in the region and the overall national effort. Officials from national leaders to emergency responders on the ground lacked the level of situational awareness necessary for a prompt and effective response to the catastrophe. This was a recipe for an inefficient and ineffective federal response.[52]

It's rare to see this type of "no BS" assessment from the federal government. Be that as it may, it doesn't change what happened as a result of those breakdowns. Lives were lost, full stop.

At this point, I imagine the question you're asking yourself is, How does this apply to me? I run a customer service team; I don't plan for hurricanes. Nothing that I do will affect nearly as many people. Well, I'm going to show you exactly how.

The Problem of Scale

Hurricane Katrina was bigger than most people expected, but—perhaps surprisingly—not actually larger than forecasted.[53] Remember the prediction by the National Weather Center? Well, they weren't wrong. You could argue that the storm's footprint was so far beyond anything that the federal government had prepared for in recent times that it's not completely surprising they were unable to provide enough aid,

---

[52] United States, Congress, "The Federal Response to Hurricane Katrina: Lessons Learned, February 2006." The Federal Response to Hurricane Katrina: Lessons Learned, February 2006, Government Printing Office, 2006, p. 41

[53] "Katrina Forecasters Were Remarkably Accurate." NBCNews.com, NBCUniversal News Group, 19 Sept. 2005, www.nbcnews.com/id/9369041/ns/us_news-katrina_the_long_road_back/t/katrina-forecasters-were-remarkably-accurate/.

resources, and manpower when it came to the immediate recovery. Prior to Katrina, you would have to go back to 1928 to identify a storm that caused more deaths. If we accept that argument, though, then we have to accept a different, no less damning premise: that emergency planners had simply become complacent when it came to disaster response planning. Which makes this a failure of people more than a failure of a system. And here's why.

When developed and deployed properly, systems can be scaled to meet the needs of all sizes, locations, and intensities. The disaster response model that everyone counted on at the time Katrina hit was rooted in common-sense actions:

- evacuate people in dangerous areas
- bring first aid to the injured
- establish lines of communication
- deploy resources appropriately

However, when a system or model is never tested beyond its typical limits, there is zero insight into what will happen once it comes under unusual or high demand. This was the Achilles' heel during Katrina: a failure to plan for the most extreme circumstances. For your team to succeed when others fail, you must account for scenarios that others deem unlikely or impossible. If it's standard practice to drill for a scenario where there is a 25 percent loss of power in a substation, have your team run the drill with a 50 percent or 85 percent loss of power. Once you reach that critical level of power loss, are you able to identify the systems that will go offline in their respective order? Will those systems be permanently damaged or repairable? How many days will it take to repair or replace those systems? These are questions you don't want to answer in the heat of the moment.

If your IT staff has created backup storage for a specific number of days, push the system out beyond that number of days and see what happens both internally and externally. Is the staff still clear-headed and focused when those storage limits are being exceeded? Will you have to dump less important information—and if so, what does that process look like? Who will need to authorize it?

These are all examples of decisions that can affect business on a micro and macro level. As the leader, your ability to plan for what *could* happen is a key component to creating a competent team that can address emergencies in real time. And it is a key component in helping your team establish the confidence to perform at a consistently high level during times of confusion and chaos. It's key because they will be prepared and ready to handle the difficult tasks. "Unexpected" will no longer be in their vocabulary.

Partnerships

As we will discuss in a later chapter, rarely is anything of significance achieved without support from other people. In the case of Katrina, the mutual aid agreements that allowed cities and states to access additional resources were of no use, though, because each jurisdiction was overwhelmed with its own disaster response. When it comes to scaling and planning, your partnerships can fall victim to the same circumstances.

Can you point to a time in the last eighteen months or less where you held strategy sessions with your partners or vendors to ensure that their capabilities are still in line with the needs of your team, division, or company? If you did, great job—you should be commended. But did you take things a step further and determine what will happen with that partner when their normal capacity is exceeded? Do they have partnerships that can be executed in short order to shore up their resources should the need arise? Who will be in charge of those additional resources? Will they expect payment before beginning work? These may seem like small issues now, but they are the types of concerns that can become problematic later and should be worked through ahead of time so that when a need arises there's no time loss. Not to mention, these issues could arise under more ordinary but still challenging circumstances, such as the loss of a partner because of contract issues or their going out of business. Have you considered that eventuality? Have you devised a plan to implement in case this happens?

One suggestion is to have members of your team cross-train with partner teams for unplanned events. The goal is not to have your team members become 100 percent knowledgeable about your partner's work functions, but for them to be functionally knowledgeable so that they can close any gaps in real time if the need occurs.

This may also require you to purchase and store materials that your partners/vendors use when they execute a task. I'm sure this may strike you as unnecessary, especially since many teams are forced to do without the supplies they need for their own roles. But we are planning for an unknown unknown here. This isn't the time to focus on saving a few dollars at the possible expense of thousands.

Lines of Communication

During the best of times open communication is a challenge for organizations, regardless of size. Now multiply that challenge across three states dealing with flooding, power outages, and the genuine fear of death, and it's a small wonder that *anything* was able to be done in the aftermath of Katrina. I admit I'm not sure how you go about recovering from a natural disaster without the ability to communicate in real time. Recovery teams that arrived in the Gulf from out of state came with their respective comms and there was little to no integration between units. There was no centralized communication plan that outlined who would direct radio traffic between parties, no designated times for communication updates, and little success in disseminating updates between civilians and local, state, and federal resources.

This communication factor, or lack thereof, was the one constant throughout the recovery effort—and it compounded all the other issues that were developing. Evacuees were dropped ad hoc at the convention center because there was no clear message to the search-and-rescue teams if they should be delivered somewhere else. Teams tasked with identifying the locations and types of damage to the levees were unable to provide feedback so that proper resources could be directed to trouble spots. Even communication to the White House was shaky. FEMA Director Michael Brown wasn't fully aware of what was happening on the ground, so his updates to the president were, of course, lacking in information. Katrina violently forced Louisiana, Mississippi, and Alabama back to a time before modern communication, and no one was fully prepared for it.

Fortunately, 99.99 percent of you will never have to prepare for a communications disaster of this size, so your strategy to work around one will be infinitely easier. Let's start with the most basic of issues: the inability to communicate with your team because phones are down. I would venture a guess that every employee has some means of cellular communication, so in the absence of landline communications making sure that you have all your employees' cell phone numbers is the first step to keeping in touch. Rather than phones being down, the more likely issue to arise is that you're not able to communicate because you're in a meeting, away on vacation, or inaccessible because of something potentially more serious, like an injury. To prepare for this, determine the member(s) of your team who will be responsible for team communication while you are absent. Go over the types of communication the team needs to function in your absence and the schedule by which the information needs to be delivered. As with all the other suggestions mentioned in this chapter, run a few test scenarios to see if everything happens the way you'd like it to. Recalibrate where necessary and move forward knowing that the team will have needed information even in your absence.

While these steps may seem elementary as you read them, I challenge you to take a moment and run through a scenario like this in your head. Ask yourself: Would your team be in the dark if you weren't able to communicate with them directly? What type of stress might this add to your team during your absence and how much of an impact would it have on their overall performance? If the answer is "no discernible effect," great—you have nothing to worry about. If that's not the case, commit to putting together a plan and share it with your team.

It would be nice to say that Katrina was an anomaly, a once-in-a-lifetime occurrence for which no lessons need be learned. But we know that it wasn't. A few years later, New York and New Jersey would be pounded by Superstorm Sandy. Twelve years later Texas and parts of Louisiana would see Hurricane Harvey arrive. Both storms presented a challenge like Katrina: heavy flooding that displaced residents and shut down utilities. State and local resources were taxed. The federal government was again called upon to provide assistance. Fortunately, many of the hard lessons learned from Katrina were put to use in these later events, and while there was still plenty to improve upon, they reflected the benefits of proper planning and execution, even for a "once-in-a-lifetime" occurrence.

Truth V

Most special operations require non-SOF assistance.

{High-performing departments require assistance from other, lesser-recognized departments}

"The main ingredient of stardom is the rest of the team." - John Wooden

The fictional city of Gotham is a world filled with henchman, criminal masterminds, and at least one sociopath. Since the 1940s that world of darkness and uncertainty has been under the watchful eye of Batman, the most famous antihero to grace the pages of modern-day storytelling. And while he's always been capable of dispensing justice in solo fashion, there's always been one person who's been essential to his alter ego and his crime-fighting persona. That man is Alfred Pennyworth.

Alfred is the man behind the man. You know the story of how a young Bruce Wayne would grow to become the masked crusader bringing justice to Gotham streets after seeing his parents murdered. What's often lost in his character arc is the fact that Bruce didn't grow to become Batman all by himself—he was always guided by the steady hand of Alfred, his guardian, caretaker, and confidante. If you remove Alfred from the picture, there's little chance that you get Batman. While the world of Batman is fictional, it perfectly illustrates the importance of the people behind the scenes. Alfred is the one who keeps up the façade; he is the one that obfuscates and misdirects when the most curious of Gotham's citizens get too close. Alfred keeps Batman focused on the big picture. His voice is one of the few that Bruce Wayne will seek counsel from, so his importance cannot be overstated. Yet his role in this world is quite understated.

For many of us here in the nonfiction world, all of this is just as true. Day in and day out, any number of unseen employees are working behind the scenes to ensure the top performers have the tools and information necessary to do their jobs at the highest level. When your top salesperson travels for a client presentation, how likely is it that his or her sales proposal is the result of a single person's effort? To be more direct, what are the odds that the presentation is the work of the salesperson alone? More often than not, it's the result of several people in multiple departments combining information to meet the client's specific needs.

In other words, it's a team effort, even if the entire team isn't placed in front of the client. What's frustrating for many of these unseen employees is the fact that most department heads, shift managers, and supervisors don't appear to be concerned about recognizing the entire team's efforts. This is too bad, because it's exactly what many employees want and need. In a 2016 article, TINYPulse, a Seattle-based maker of employee engagement software, rounded up a list of statistics showing the importance of offering support for *all* employees. Here's what they found:

- In a poll asking employees what leaders could do to improve engagement, 58 percent of respondents replied "give recognition."
- 50 percent of employees surveyed in another poll believed being thanked by managers not only improved their relationship but also builds trust with their higher-ups.
- According to one study, companies with recognition programs that are highly effective at improving employee engagement have 31 percent lower voluntary turnover.[54]

Recognition is all that most people want. It's not necessary for them to become the face of the company; they simply want their work to be recognized with the same level of enthusiasm as the company's "shining stars." In the spirit of offering credit where it's due, in this final chapter we're going to look at the efforts of some incredibly talented individuals whose "behind the scenes" work contributed to others' enormous success. There's no better illustration of this process than in the music industry, so it will be my focus. The figures profiled here propelled a generation of musicians into stardom and created legacies that will continue for decades to come.

* * *

The Wrecking Crew

If you grew up dancing to the pop music of the mid-1960s and '70s, boy do I have some news for you. It might even change the way you see artists from that time period. Ready? Here it is: *The music you loved so dearly was rarely created by your favorite artists.* When you saw it performed live, they were, in fact, playing the music—but they were not the originators of the sound. The overwhelming majority of your favorite songs were created by a collective of studio musicians known as "the Wrecking Crew." If you aren't familiar with studio musicians, these are artists hired by record companies and producers to provide the musical backdrop for recordings. They are hired because of their incredible

---

[54] https://www.tinypulse.com/blog/sk-employee-recognition-stats

musicianship and ability to translate the producer's vision into a song that's enjoyable to everyone. During the '60s and "70s, this skillset was essential for many record labels because it allowed them to package acts visually without being terribly concerned about how their music would sound. The Wrecking Crew would make sure it sounded great.

Now that we have that dirty little secret out of the way, let's talk about music for a bit. Do you remember the song "Good Vibrations" by the Beach Boys? If you do that's excellent. If not, have Siri or Bixby play it for you and take note of the bassline. Now I have a question for you, who was the original bass player for that song?

To be fair, this is a trick question. The original bass player was a rhythmic virtuoso named Carol Kaye. You'd be forgiven for not knowing who she is, the irony is, she was one of the most sought-after musicians of that era. The melody that so many of you have come to associate with that summer was plucked out by her skillful fingers. She would go on to record hundreds of songs and provide basslines for multiple number-one albums. With that much talent, you might ask, why was she such a hidden figure? Simple. As I mentioned earlier, the record labels had to market their groups to the younger generation. During that time young, good-looking guys sold records; talented female musicians didn't. Brian Wilson may be credited with writing the music to "Good Vibrations," but Kaye is the one who brought the notes to life. She also provided the bassline for another Beach Boys hit you may have heard of,

"California Girls." Which made her a star in her own right amongst those in the know.

The Wrecking Crew consisted of ten to twelve musicians who would all go on to leave their mark on the music world. As a point of reference, here are just a few artists whose original music was recorded by the group: the Monkees, the Carpenters, Gary Lewis & the Playboys, Jan and Dean, the Association, the Grass Roots, Simon & Garfunkel, Paul Revere & the Raiders, Kenny Rogers and the First Edition, and the Mamas and the Papas.[55] We are talking about a decade-plus of music that can be traced back to a small group of highly talented but hidden artists. They were rarely if ever credited on the actual songs. Of course, they were compensated, but there was no outward recognition of their talents. To do so would risk casting doubt about the musicianship of the stars record companies had invested so much time and money into.

Many of you reading this might notice some similarities to the situation with your teams or in your office. Top billing for a project or presentation typically goes to the darlings of the company, the favored faces. Yet, behind the scenes, tucked away in a conference room far out of sight, you'll find teams of committed individuals putting their natural skills to work for the larger team goal. Many of them do so with full knowledge that their individual efforts may go unrecognized.

---

[55] Hartman, Kent. "The Wrecking Crew." AMERICAN HERITAGE, Feb. 2007, www.americanheritage.com/content/wrecking-crew.

Now some of you may argue that these supporting cast members were paid, so what's the issue? If you're looking at this from a purely financial standpoint, your argument is spot-on. The members of the Wrecking Crew were compensated, most of them quite well in fact. However, as with most things in life, there's more at stake. Let me ask you a question. Did you ever pick up a guitar because of the Beach Boys or the Monkees? Were you part of a band that patterned themselves after these groups? It's a safe bet the sounds of those bands inspired many to pursue a career in music. Now think of all those who didn't try their hand in music because they didn't match the perfectly styled image of these and other popular groups of the time. It's a bit of a double-edged sword when you think about it. The talent typically creates the platform for the image to take root and grow. Unfortunately, the image begins to overshadow the talent and people simply want to emulate the image, not the talent. We're always told to model what works, so the question you must start asking is, are we modeling the right people?

This is where your role as a leader begins. Your understanding of team dynamics will lay the groundwork for success or failure. Your team needs to be exposed to everything and *everyone* that goes into these successes and failures. Too much emphasis on starring roles can lead to unchecked egos, while failing to provide recognition of supporting roles can lead to team members jumping ship. Striking a healthy balance will be key. To that point, let's discuss a few strategies that can assist you in this important leadership area.

Lift Every Voice

As television became more prevalent during the '60s and '70s it became clear that the image of any up-and-coming recording star was going to be a considerable factor in their popularity. So it stands to reason that the record labels focused more of their attention on the visual aspect of the groups it signed and promoted. While their images help drive sales and generate legions of fans, in several cases it was nothing more than a veneer. In reality many of these "stars" had only basic songwriting and playing skills. But the labels and producers knew they had a pool of accomplished musicians in the background who could translate the simplest of music into a bona fide hit, so the process worked. Once you have the music, all you need is a face to show the public. With this in mind, consider for a moment the thousands of young men that would have been influenced by the image of the Beach Boys. I imagine sales of guitars would have skyrocketed during their peak popularity.

Now imagine the opposite of this—what the impact on aspiring female musicians would have been had they been exposed to Carol Kaye at the height of her musical career. Would we have seen an all-female version of the Beach Boys? Consider for a moment how much wider the talent pool could have been if more women were exposed to the Wrecking Crew and their work. In 2016, the story of the black female mathematicians who worked behind their white male counterparts at NASA during the early stages of the space race came to the big screen in the aptly named movie *Hidden Figures*, introducing an entire generation of little girls to a world that had been hidden from them. Now the names Katherine Johnson, Mary Jackson, and Dorothy Vaughan stand out as shining examples for women irrespective of age, ethnicity, or career field.

As an astute leader, you'll recognize that inspiration is a tool that is regularly mentioned but often narrowly employed. Meaning, we know our teams need to be inspired to push for larger goals, but we don't always know what that inspiration should look like or where it should come from. It's easy to underestimate the amount of inspiration that can come from the simple act of recognizing team members, but it's a skill that you will need to learn. When your team members see that all the work done by the team is equally awarded and appreciated, you create an environment where everyone wants to participate. Your team becomes a destination for everyone who wants to be part of something different. When more people want to participate, the potential upside is tremendous and the work that can come from your team grows exponentially. Imagine how the senior leaders of your organization begin to view you when your team becomes a center of influence. Which leads us to my next point.

Win-Win

In a traditional win-win scenario, both sides come away with a sense of having accomplished something significant. No one feels slighted, ignored, or like they were forced to take a losing position. Unfortunately, many consider today's workplace to be a win-lose scenario, where one party must lose for another party to win. If you doubt this view is prevalent among workers, a 2018 study conducted by Randstad USA should clear all of that up for you. Consider the following three takeaways about career potential that come from the study:

- 58 percent of surveyed workers agreed their companies don't currently have enough growth opportunities for them to stay longer term.
- 69 percent said they would be more satisfied if their employers better utilized their skills and abilities.
- More than half (57 percent) said they need to leave their current company in order to take their careers to the next level.[56]

What does all this mean for you as a current frontline leader or future senior leader? It's clear that employees are becoming more proactive when it comes to the development of their careers. They aren't waiting for someone to retire or something more drastic to happen before they get their chance to move on to new roles. Underappreciated employees will leave for better opportunities. And with each departure, there will be a temporary loss of team strength, chemistry, and overall effectiveness. If too many of the supporting members leave, you risk having staff who may not be willing or capable of stepping into a supporting role.

---

[56] https://www.randstadusa.com/about/news/your-best-employees-are-leaving-but-is-it-personal-or-practical/

Now let's assume you've been paying attention to all the data and you've been hard at work at addressing the lack of recognition. You've mapped your actions to reflect this and your team regularly rates higher in job satisfaction and lower in employee turnover. You're off to a head start and may even have been allowed by senior management to experiment with other methods that can be duplicated throughout your company. What steps can you take to foster this win-win environment? Let me suggest a formula that may be helpful:

R + O = G | (Recognition + Opportunity = Growth)

Recognition. Part of being the leader is making sure that employees are recognized for their contributions. This recognition can be internal or external, made on an individual basis or as part of a larger effort. The act of recognizing work reinforces to employees that they bring value to the team, and a happy by-product of this can be an increase in employee confidence. That increase can then lead employees to take on larger or more complex roles.

Opportunity. In too many cases we view opportunities for employees in a linear fashion. We see their career path only as it exists in the organizational chart. Too often, we don't think broadly enough when it comes to generating opportunities. Employee A will start at the bottom rung of their career path and will view their growth through the rubric you provide. At each new stage, they will look to you for guidance. And like most companies, you'll consider it—only when you are forced to. Thinking creatively opens up different possibilities, though. It allows you to be proactive instead of reactive.

As an example, lateral transfers into new departments or roles are great for employees who need a new challenge or may have reached the top of their salary band. This has the potential of reinvigorating an employee who might have found themselves becoming bored at work. It may also recapture an employee who is actively looking to leave the organization. Remember that 57 percent mentioned above?

If lateral transfers aren't available, leveraging special projects inside the organization may provide another way to highlight an employee's skills. Even if their contributions are made outside of their primary department, this kind of arrangement helps serve the corporation at large and show your employees that you are genuinely interested in participating in the growth of their career. For too long the trend has been to do what's in your best interest as a manager first. But you have the opportunity to bend the curve and show other managers the benefits of putting team members first, thereby becoming a standard-bearer for your peers.

Growth. The growth of an employee should not be something left to HR. It is not something you focus on once a year during annual reviews. An employee's growth inside the organization is not an accidental event. To date, I don't know of anyone who accidentally became the head of marketing or a senior sales rep or project management officer. Ascending into those roles is the result of planning, open discussions, and hard work. As we move forward, let's all agree to the truth of the following statement: "Employee growth is the result of an *intentional collaborative* effort between an employee and their leadership team." As a leader, this means you will need to develop the skill and desire to grow multiple careers in addition to your own; if you want to separate your team and yourself from your peers in the office. Remember, nearly 60 percent of employees don't think their employers have long term plans for them. Will you be the exception to this statistic?

It's probably in your best interest to be the exception and here's why. If HR or the senior leaders came to you and asked if you could identify the members of your team most likely to leave, would you be able to do it? Is it your second-in-command, who keeps the team on task in your absence? Maybe your most creative team member? Or even worse, the team member who has all the real connections inside the building? In any case, just one of these losses would be significant to your team. Now imagine more than one. How do you recover?

In the previous chapters I've shared what the world could look like for your employees if you just decided to do things a little differently. More creativity, better team cohesion and less employee turnover, but the lesson in this one is a no-brainer. We all look for some form of recognition. Though we may not broadcast it regularly, that doesn't mean we are perfectly fine to live a life without it. The psychologist Abraham Maslow famously identified this in his hierarchy of needs:

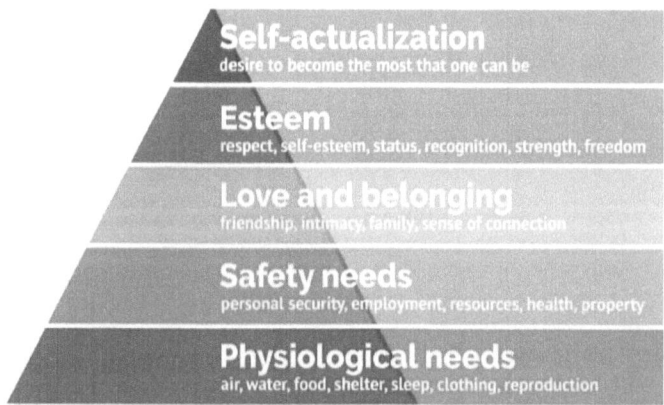

Right there at the number-two spot is status, recognition, and respect. That's all anyone ever asks for, and you as a leader occupy the perfect position to ensure these needs are met. Remember there was a time when you too sought the approval, respect, and admiration of those above you. Truth be told, while your title may have changed, the need likely still remains for you as well. So think of all those people behind the scenes who feel the same.

Notes

Genesis

1.
"Bridging the Skills Gap: Workforce Development and the Future of Work," December 2018, pg. 12, Amy Souza and Kristen Fyfe-Mills Nancy Harvin, Jerry Kaminski, Cristina Masucci, and Paul Smith.

2.
2018 Leadership Forecast Development Dimensions International (DDI), pg. 4, "Global Leadership Forecast 2018 - 25 Research Insights to Fuel Your People Strategy," 2018, pg. 4 Rebecca L. Ray

3.
"State of the Global Workplace - Employee Engagement Insights for Business Leaders Worldwide," Ed O'Boyle, Jim Harter PhD, pg 12

4.
"State of the American Workplace," Gallup pg. 17

5.
"State of the American Workplace," Gallup pg. 6

6.
"State of the American Workplace," Gallup pg. 9

Truth I

7.
https://www.brookings.edu/wp-content/uploads/2019/01/2019.01_BrookingsMetro_Automation-AI_Report_Muro-Maxim-Whiton-FINAL-version.pdf, in "Executive Summary" section.

8.
Interview with the author. Taken from an interview with Eduardo Sanchez in September 2015

9.
"Shift Change: 'Just-in-Time' Scheduling Creates Chaos for Workers." NBCNews.com, NBCUniversal News Group, 10 May 2014, www.nbcnews.com/feature/in-plain-sight/shift-change-just-in-time-scheduling-creates-chaos-workers-n95881.

10.
Ibid.
11.
Tsosie, Claire. "Just-In-Time Scheduling: Does It Really Save Companies Money?" NerdWallet, 24 Sept.
2014, www.nerdwallet.com/blog/finance/time-scheduling-save-companies-money/
12.
"Short Shifted." http://retailactionproject.org/wp-content/uploads/2014/09/ShortShifted_report_FINAL.pdf
13.
"Discounted Jobs." http://retailactionproject.org/wp-content/uploads/2012/01/FINAL_RAP.pdf
14.
"Shift Change: 'Just-in-Time' Scheduling Creates Chaos for Workers." NBCNews.com, NBCUniversal News Group, May 10,
2014, www.nbcnews.com/feature/in-plain-sight/shift-change-just-in-time-scheduling-creates-chaos-workers-n95881.
15.
Ibid.
16.
https://cdn.americanprogress.org/wp-content/uploads/2012/11/CostofTurnover.pdf pg 3
17.
https://cdn.americanprogress.org/wp-content/uploads/2012/11/CostofTurnover.pdf pg 2

Truth II

18.
https://www.mercedes-amg.com/en/driving-performance/history.html
19.
https://rmsothebys.com/en/auctions/am19/amelia-island/lots/r0026-1989-mercedes-benz-560-sec-amg-60-wide-body/733351.
20.

https://www.mercedes-amg.com/en/driving-performance/history.html.
21.
https://newatlas.com/keanu-reeves-arch-motorcycle-company-krgt-1/34360
22.
https://www.bloomberg.com/news/articles/2016-08-15/keanu-reeves-will-build-a-78-000-arch-motorcycle-just-for-you
23.
Ibid
24.
Ibid
25.
https://whatis.techtarget.com/definition/Parkinsons-law-of-triviality-bikeshedding
26.
https://www.hotcars.com/why-is-everyone-talking-about-keanu-reeves-motorcycle-company/
27.
https://www.rideapart.com/articles/245086/keanus-not-so-death-defying-super-bowl-ad/

Truth III

28.
https://www.fool.com/investing/2017/06/01/5-key-moments-in-berkshire-hathaway-stock-history.aspx
29.
http://masonmyers.com/berkshire-hathaway-management-structure/
30.
https://www.multpl.com/s-p-500-historical-prices/table/by-year
31.
https://www.macrotrends.net/stocks/charts/KO/coca-cola/stock-price-history

32.
https://www.cnbc.com/2019/01/31/warren-buffett-on-his-successful-relationship-with-charlie-munger.html
33.
Ibid.
34.
https://fortune.com/2018/05/07/warren-buffett-four-successors
35.
https://www.bls.gov/news.release/tenure.nr0.htm
36.
https://hbr.org/2013/12/the-hidden-benefits-of-keeping-teams-intact.
37.
https://positivepsychologyprogram.com/psychology-teamwork.
38.
Ibid.
39.
https://rework.withgoogle.com/print/guides/5721312655835136/
40.
Ibid.
41.
https://papers.ssrn.com/sol3/papers.cfm?abstract_id=2678556, p. 2
42.
https://papers.ssrn.com/sol3/papers.cfm?abstract_id=2678556, p. 1

Truth IV

43. History.com Staff. "Hurricane Katrina." History.com, A&E Television Networks, 2009, www.history.com/topics/hurricane-katrina.
44.
Ibid.
45.
United States, Congress, "The Federal Response to Hurricane Katrina: Lessons Learned, February 2006." The Federal Response to Hurricane

Katrina: Lessons Learned, February 2006, Government Printing Office, 2006, p.7

46.
United States, Congress, "The Federal Response to Hurricane Katrina: Lessons Learned, February 2006." The Federal Response to Hurricane Katrina: Lessons Learned, February 2006, Government Printing Office, 2006, p.8

47.
United States, Congress, "The Federal Response to Hurricane Katrina: Lessons Learned, February 2006." The Federal Response to Hurricane Katrina: Lessons Learned, February 2006, Government Printing Office, 2006, p. 14

48.
United States, Congress, "The Federal Response to Hurricane Katrina: Lessons Learned, February 2006." The Federal Response to Hurricane Katrina: Lessons Learned, February 2006, Government Printing Office, 2006, p. 34

49.
United States, Congress, "The Federal Response to Hurricane Katrina: Lessons Learned, February 2006." The Federal Response to Hurricane Katrina: Lessons Learned, February 2006, Government Printing Office, 2006, p. 37

50.
United States, Congress, "The Federal Response to Hurricane Katrina: Lessons Learned, February 2006." The Federal Response to Hurricane Katrina: Lessons Learned, February 2006, Government Printing Office, 2006, p. 29

51.
United States, Congress, "The Federal Response to Hurricane Katrina: Lessons Learned, February 2006." The Federal Response to Hurricane Katrina: Lessons Learned, February 2006, Government Printing Office, 2006, p. 30

52.
United States, Congress, "The Federal Response to Hurricane Katrina: Lessons Learned, February 2006." The Federal Response to Hurricane Katrina: Lessons Learned, February 2006, Government Printing Office, 2006, p. 41

53.

"Katrina Forecasters Were Remarkably Accurate." NBCNews.com, NBCUniversal News Group, 19 Sept.
2005, www.nbcnews.com/id/9369041/ns/us_news-katrina_the_long_road_back/t/katrina-forecasters-were-remarkably-accurate/.

Truth V

54.
https://www.tinypulse.com/blog/sk-employee-recognition-stats
55.
Hartman, Kent. "The Wrecking Crew." AMERICAN HERITAGE, Feb.
2007, www.americanheritage.com/content/wrecking-crew.
56.
https://www.randstadusa.com/about/news/your-best-employees-are-leaving-but-is-it-personal-or-practical/

www.ingramcontent.com/pod-product-compliance
Lightning Source LLC
Chambersburg PA
CBHW021446210526
45463CB00002B/648